Serving America's Veterans

Recent Titles in
Contemporary Military, Strategic, and Security Issues

Intelligence and National Security: A Reference Handbook
J. Ransom Clark

Military Reform: A Reference Handbook
Winslow T. Wheeler and Lawrence J. Korb

The U.S. Military's "Don't Ask, Don't Tell" Policy: A Reference Handbook
Melissa Sheridan Embser-Herbert

Prisoners of War: A Reference Handbook
Arnold Krammer

Nation-Building and Stability Operations: A Reference Handbook
Cynthia A. Watson

Military Transformation and Modern Warfare: A Reference Handbook
Elinor Sloan

Information Operations—Doctrine and Practice: A Reference Handbook
Christopher Paul

The National Guard and Reserve: A Reference Handbook
Michael D. Doubler

Returning Wars' Wounded, Injured, and Ill: A Reference Handbook
Nathan D. Ainspan and Walter E. Penk, editors

Manning the Future Legions of the United States: Finding and Developing Tomorrow's Centurions
Donald Vandergriff

The Process and Politics of Defense Acquisition: A Reference Handbook
David S. Sorenson

International Crime and Punishment: A Guide to the Issues
James Larry Taulbee

Serving America's Veterans

A Reference Handbook

Lawrence J. Korb, Sean E. Duggan,
Peter M. Juul, and Max A. Bergmann

Contemporary Military, Strategic, and Security Issues

PRAEGER SECURITY INTERNATIONAL
An Imprint of ABC-CLIO, LLC

A B C CLIO

Santa Barbara, California • Denver, Colorado • Oxford, England

Copyright 2009 by Lawrence J. Korb, Sean E. Duggan, Peter M. Juul, Max A. Bergmann

Library of Congress Cataloging-in-Publication Data

Serving America's veterans : a reference handbook / Lawrence J. Korb .. [et al.].
    p. cm. — (Contemporary military, strategic, and security issues)
   Includes bibliographical references and index.
   ISBN 978-0-313-35526-4 (hardcover : alk. paper) —
   ISBN 978-0-313-35527-1 (ebook)
  1. Veterans—Services for—United States—Handbooks, manuals, etc.   2. Veterans—Medical care—United States—Handbooks, manuals, etc.   3. Veterans—Mental health services—United States—Handbooks, manuals, etc.   4. United States. Dept. of Veterans Affairs—Handbooks, manuals, etc.   I. Korb, Lawrence J., 1939–
   UB357.S47   2009
   362.0860973—dc22   2009016478

13 12 11 10 9   1 2 3 4 5

This book is also available on the World Wide Web as an eBook.
Visit www.abc-clio.com for details.

ABC-CLIO, LLC
130 Cremona Drive, P.O. Box 1911
Santa Barbara, California 93116–1911

This book is printed on acid-free paper (∞)

Manufactured in the United States of America

To the Soldiers, Sailors, Airmen, Marines, and Coast Guardsmen
who volunteer or were drafted to defend our country.

The willingness with which our young people are likely to serve in
any war, no matter how justified, shall be directly proportional to how
they perceive veterans of earlier wars were treated and appreciated by
our nation.

—George Washington

Contents

Preface   ix

Chapter 1   Introduction   1
                 Lawrence J. Korb

Chapter 2   The History of Veterans Affairs   15
                 Peter M. Juul

Chapter 3   The Impact of Veterans on the American
                 Political System   51
                 Max A. Bergmann

Chapter 4   Veteran Demographics: Today's Population,
                 Tomorrow's Projections   93
                 Sean E. Duggan

Chapter 5   Administrative Barriers to Accessing VA Health
                 Care and Benefits   113
                 Sean E. Duggan

Chapter 6   Multiple Epidemics in Veteran Mental Health   139
                 Sean E. Duggan

Chapter 7   Conclusion   155
                 Lawrence J. Korb

Index   159

Preface

With the appointment of General Erik Shinseki to head the Department of Veterans Affairs (VA), President Barack Obama made it clear that the needs of all veterans, particularly those who suffered physical and mental wounds, would be a high priority in his administration. General Shinseki is arguably the most distinguished person ever appointed to head the Department of Veterans Affairs or its precursor, the Veterans Administration.

General Shinseki, a native Hawaiian, graduated from West Point in 1965, served two combat tours in Vietnam, first as an artillery forward observer and then as a cavalry troop commander. During his time in Vietnam, the General was wounded twice, once so severely that he lost his foot. As a result, the army wanted to discharge this wounded veteran but Shinseki pleaded to remain on active duty and the army, which was hemorrhaging experienced officers as a result of Vietnam, agreed.

Over the next 35 years, General Shinseki rose through the ranks in army command and staff positions. He commanded the 1st Cavalry Division in 1994 and 1995 and led NATO forces in Bosnia from 1997 to 1998. In 1999, President Clinton appointed him as the 34th Chief of Staff of the U.S. Army.

During his time in office, General Shinseki has displayed the same type of courage that he had shown on the battlefield. During the lead-up to the invasion of Iraq in 2003, General Shinseki told the Senate Armed Services Committee that several hundred thousand troops would be needed to occupy and stabilize Iraq after the fall of Saddam Hussein, rather than the 30,000 the Bush administration had been planning on.

For his candor, the General was ridiculed by members of the Bush administration, including Deputy Secretary of Defense Paul Wolfowitz, a Vietnam draft evader. Wolfowitz said that it was ridiculous to argue that more troops would be needed after the war than during the war. Moreover, none of Shinseki's colleagues on the Joint Chiefs of Staff came to his defense either publicly or privately.

By ignoring Shinseki's advice, the Bush administration allowed Iraq to devolve into chaos after the fall of Saddam. As a result, over 4,000 young men and women needlessly lost their lives and over 30,000 suffered physical wounds and other 300,000 suffered mental wounds.

Shinseki also proved prophetic in warning the Bush administration that trying to wage two wars with an active duty force composed of less than 500,000 people and 10 combat divisions would place an unfair and immoral strain on these brave men and women. As General Shinseki noted, trying to implement a 12 division strategy with a 10 division Army would mean that troops would not receive enough time between deployments to combat areas and that other troops would be rushed into battle without sufficient individual or unit training.

But the Bush administration and Secretary of Defense Donald Rumsfeld resisted Shinseki's advice. In their view, technology could substitute for manpower and Rumsfeld actually wanted to reduce the active Army from 10 to 8 divisions. Moreover, accepting Shinseki's recommendations would mean that the mission in Iraq would not be accomplished quickly.

Shinseki was vindicated in early 2007 when President Bush, under pressure from Congress and the Joint Chiefs of Staff, agreed to increase the size of the Army permanently from 485,000 active soldiers to 550,000.

During his confirmation hearing to head the Department of Veterans Affairs, General Shinseki made it clear that he would bring the same insights and candor to that agency as he did to the Army. He pledged to transform the VA into a proactive "21st-century organization to meet the needs of a growing population of wounded veterans." He pledged to speed up the sluggish process for approving claims that commonly take an average of six months; to streamline the transfer of medical and other records from the Defense Department to the VA; to better meet the needs of veterans living in rural areas; and to modernize the delivery of benefits. His message to veterans was that he would treat them with the respect and dignity that they deserve and not consider them as beggars looking for a handout.

There is no doubt that President Obama's selection of General Shinseki, who is himself an amputee, will inspire confidence in military veterans. As former Republican presidential candidate and Senate Majority Leader, Robert J. Dole, also a severely wounded veteran, put it at Shinseki's confirmation hearing, "here's a man who has been through it; here's a man who understands." And as this volume will make clear, at this time in our history, the VA needs someone who understands if the nation's 24 million veterans are to receive the care and benefits they have earned.

CHAPTER 1

Introduction

Lawrence J. Korb

The U.S. government has asked its citizens to volunteer or has drafted them to fight this nation's wars since the country's inception. From the Revolutionary War against the British to the conflicts currently being waged in Iraq and Afghanistan, some 100 million men and women have taken up arms in the defense of the United States. As our first president and first commander in chief George Washington noted, "the willingness with which our young people are likely to serve in any war, no matter how justified, shall be directly proportional to how they perceive veterans of earlier wars are appreciated by our nation."

Proper appreciation of our veterans must involve more than welcome home parades or bumper stickers on cars; it must also involve treating the physical wounds suffered while in service and the mental problems resulting from the stress of combat as well as helping these men and women make a successful transition back to civilian life.

Veterans of all wars have faced these challenges. However, the nearly two million veterans returning from the wars in Iraq and Afghanistan who have left or been forced to leave the military face unique challenges. These challenges are a result of at least nine factors that are unique to this group of servicemen and women and the wars they are fighting.

First, this is the first long war or extended conflict that has been fought by an all-volunteer force (AVF). Since the end of conscription in 1973, the United States has conducted several military operations. However, prior to 2001, all of the campaigns have been relatively short or moved quickly from combat operations to peace enforcement or peacekeeping.

The attempted rescue of the American hostages from Iran in 1980, though it ended tragically, lasted but two days. The peace enforcement operation in Lebanon in 1983, which resulted in the deaths of 241 marines in October of that year, ended within six months of that tragedy. The invasion of Grenada that same month ended within a couple of days, as did the operation to overthrow Noriega in Panama in 1989.

While the United States sent some 500,000 troops to the Persian Gulf in 1991 to liberate Kuwait, that war was over very quickly. It took 37 days of sustained bombing and 100 hours of ground combat to evict the Iraqi forces of Saddam Hussein from Kuwait. Similarly, the major combat operations in Bosnia in 1994 and Kosovo in 1999 did not involve significant ground combat and lasted only a few weeks before transitioning to peace enforcement and peacekeeping.

In contrast, the wars in Iraq and Afghanistan have dragged on for more than six and eight years, respectively, with no end in sight, and still involve continuing combat operations resulting in casualties.

Second, this is the first war since the end of World War II in which military people not only must undergo multiple deployments but also do not receive adequate rest—or what the military calls dwell-time—between deployments, or sufficient training before being sent to combat. The wars in Korea and Vietnam were fought primarily with draftees. In each of those wars, men were conscripted for no more than two years. Normally, they received one year of training before they were sent to Korea or Vietnam for a year, after which they were discharged.

Very few of those who decided to make the military a career served more than two tours involuntarily in either Korea or Vietnam, even though the later conflict lasted almost a decade. Moreover, those careerists who did return to Korea or Vietnam for a second tour normally received at least two years at home before returning to the combat zone, at least one year to recuperate from the rigors of combat and another to train to go back. For example, General Colin Powell, who entered the army in the late 1950s, served two one-year tours as a junior and middle grade officer during the decade the army and the nation were involved in Vietnam.

This has not been the case in Iraq and Afghanistan. Virtually every army combat unit or brigade combat team has already had multiple tours to one or both of these theaters. Moreover, because our ground forces are so small relative to the demands the Pentagon has had to place upon them, the Department of Defense has had to break its social compact with its soldiers and marines. This compact says that for every day a serviceman or woman spends in a combat zone, he or she will spend at least two days at home.

Thus, if a soldier spends 12 or 15 months in Iraq or Afghanistan, there should not be further combat requirements until he or she has been home for 24 or 30 months. But since 9/11, thousands of soldiers have been sent back into combat with only a year at home after serving 12 to 15 months, some with much less than a year. In fact, in 2007, when Congress passed a law saying that military personnel should spend a minimum of one day at home for every day deployed, President Bush was forced to veto it so that he could maintain the number of troops he felt were needed in Iraq and Afghanistan.

Finally, in order to meet the manpower needs of units being sent back to Iraq and Afghanistan, the Pentagon has sent many people with physical and mental problems into the war zone and many new recruits have been sent into combat with only a few months of training rather than the normal year.

For example, in order to fill the ranks, the army pressed 79 injured soldiers into duty in Iraq in December of 2007. The soldiers from Fort Carson, Colorado, were deployed to Kuwait and Iraq while they were still receiving medical treatment for various conditions.[1] According to an article by Mark Benjamin in *Salon* magazine, as the Pentagon was struggling to man the five combat brigades that were to be part of the surge in Iraq, a unit of the army's 3rd Infantry Division at Fort Benning, Georgia, deployed troops with "serious injuries and other medical problems, including GIs who doctors have said [were] medically unfit for battle. Some [were] too injured to wear their body armor, according to medical records."[2]

Mark Benjamin also stated:

> On Feb. 15, Master Sgt. Jenkins and 74 other soldiers with medical conditions from the 3rd Division's 3rd Brigade were summoned to a meeting with the division surgeon and brigade surgeon. These are the men responsible for handling each soldier's "physical profile," an Army document that lists for commanders an injured soldier's physical limitations because of medical problems—from being unable to fire a weapon to the inability to move and dive in three-to-five-second increments to avoid enemy fire. Jenkins and other soldiers claim that the division and brigade surgeons summarily downgraded soldiers' profiles, without even a medical exam, in order to deploy them to Iraq. It is a claim division officials deny.[3]

Similarly, anecdotal evidence suggests that soldiers are being rushed into combat without proper training time. One week after deploying to Iraq, 18-year-old Private Matthew Zeimer's outpost in Ramadi was attacked by insurgents. During a gun battle, Zeimer and a fellow soldier were killed. It was the private's first assignment to a combat post in Iraq. According to Mark Thompson of *Time* magazine:

> If Zeimer's combat career was brief, so was his training. He enlisted last June at age 17, three weeks after graduating from Dawson County

High School in eastern Montana. After finishing nine weeks of basic training and additional preparation in infantry tactics in Oklahoma, he arrived at Fort Stewart, Ga., in early December. But Zeimer had missed the intense four-week pre-Iraq training—a taste of what troops will face in combat—that his 1st Brigade comrades got at their home post in October. Instead, Zeimer and about 140 other members of the 4,000-strong brigade got a cut-rate, 10-day course on weapon use, first aid and Iraqi culture. That's the same length as the course that teaches soldiers assigned to generals' household staffs the finer points of table service.[4]

Third, the reserve component (National Guard and reserves) has been used as an operational rather than a strategic reserve. When the nation ended the draft and decided to rely on the AVF to protect the nation, it created an AVF with three components: a comparatively small active force to handle small wars and peacekeeping operations; a guard and reserve that would serve as a bridge to the reinstitution of the draft for extended conflicts; and the creation of a pool of potential military personnel formed by having all young men register for the draft when they turned 18.

But since neither political party nor any branch of government has the political will to tap into this pool by reinstituting the draft, the reserve component, rather than serving as a bridge to conscription, now has become an operational reserve alternating combat deployments with the active force. Since 9/11, virtually all of the Army National Guard's enhanced combat brigades have been mobilized and deployed to Iraq and Afghanistan on multiple occasions. Many supporting units have also been mobilized repeatedly. In 2005, 46 percent (or about 60,000) of the troops in Iraq were from the reserve component.[5]

This was not the case in our previous extended conflicts. In fact, during the war in Vietnam, President Johnson, fearful of sparking opposition to the war, decided not to mobilize the reserve component. Instead, he chose to expand the size of the active army with draftees. And while the reserves were mobilized to fight in Korea, no units or individuals were compelled to serve more than one 12-month tour.

When these reservists, who have been mobilized to fight what President Bush calls the Global War on Terror (GWOT), finish their tours in Iraq or Afghanistan, they lose their military health benefits and are thrown back into the civilian healthcare system. Moreover, since 20 percent of the men and women in the Guard and reserves do not have medical coverage in their civilian jobs, they must look elsewhere for treatment, particularly for mental problems that often do not manifest themselves until some time after they return from combat and are released from active duty. Even those who do have coverage are often enrolled in health care plans that do not cover their war injuries.

Finally, using the reserves in an operational as opposed to a strategic role means that the Pentagon has had to break its social compact with them as well. This compact says that no reservist will be mobilized more than one year out of every five. But, as indicated above, since 9/11 several Guard and reserve units have not only been mobilized several times, but some have served nearly two years on active duty.

Fourth, this is the first conflict in which women have been habitually exposed to close combat. After the first Persian Gulf War, Congress repealed most of the restrictions that prevented women from serving in combat positions. Since 1991, women have been allowed to fly combat aircraft and helicopters, serve on combat ships, and be assigned to ground combat units. The only restriction is that a woman cannot be assigned to frontline ground combat components (armor, artillery, and infantry) that are expected to engage in direct combat. However, in the insurgencies being fought in Iraq and Afghanistan, there are no front lines and women assigned to support units like logistics, military police, civil affairs, and intelligence have been exposed to as much danger as any frontline combat component.

Not surprisingly, of the hundreds of thousands of women sent to Iraq and Afghanistan through the end of 2008, more than 100 have been killed and another 1,000 wounded. To compound the problem, about 15 percent of the women serving in Iraq and Afghanistan have experienced sexual trauma during their deployment, and many more have been victims of sexual harassment and assault. Women who have experienced sexual trauma are three times more likely to be diagnosed with mental illnesses than those who did not.

Fifth, because of advances in medical care, the chances of a military person surviving his or her wounds today compared to previous wars have increased markedly. In Iraq and Afghanistan the ratio of wounded in combat to killed is 15 to 1. By way of contrast, in Vietnam the ratio of wounded to killed in combat was 2.6 to 1. In World War II it was 2 to 1. This means that compared to previous wars, many more severely wounded veterans will return home and need extended care.

Sixth, waging long wars that have become increasingly unpopular with the American people has meant that the army, in particular, has had to lower its standards for attracting and retaining sufficient volunteers to wage these conflicts. To meet its recruiting goals, it has been forced to lower its educational and aptitude standards. While the army aims to have over 90 percent of its recruits with a high school diploma or equivalent, in FY 2008 that number was 83 percent, and in FY 2007 it was 79 percent.

Similarly, the army has had to grant thousands of waivers each year to fill its ranks. In 2004, the percentage of army recruits with so-called moral waivers was 12 percent. That number rose to 18 percent in the final four months of FY 2008.[6]

Consequently, the army has had to take in individuals with physical and mental problems that are exacerbated when they are exposed to the pressures and rigors of combat. To keep their units filled, the army has also reduced the failure rate in basic training by half, thus sending people into war zones who should and normally would have been weeded out in basic training as unfit to serve.

In addition, because of these repeated deployments without sufficient time at home, retention of high quality noncommissioned and commissioned officers has suffered. As a result, virtually all E-4s are promoted to E-5 and all captains to major when they have sufficient time in grade. This means that the people leading the troops into battle today are often not of the same high quality as those who performed similar roles in Korea or Vietnam or the first Persian Gulf War, or at the beginning of the conflicts in Iraq and Afghanistan.

Seventh, this is the first extended conflict in which the army and marines have deployed whole units rather than individuals. In Korea and Vietnam, soldiers and marines spent a year with the unit that remained in the theater for the duration of the conflict. In Iraq and Afghanistan, the whole brigade or combat team comes and goes as a unit. While this deployment pattern may enhance unit cohesion, it comes at a cost to many individuals. Once a unit is notified that it will be deployed to Iraq or Afghanistan, all its members must remain on active duty until three months after the unit returns home from the theater. To keep the units fully staffed, the Pentagon has had to invoke stop loss (the involuntary extension of a service member's active duty service under the enlistment contract in order to retain them beyond their initial end of term of service date) for over 120,000 people. In September of 2008 alone, 12,200 soldiers were affected by stop loss; the same number likely will be affected each month through 2009.[7]

Consequently, some soldiers must remain on duty for up to two years after their enlistment was due to expire, thus forcing them to put their plans to return to civilian life on hold and adding to the stress of combat and family separation.

Eighth, the GWOT is being waged by a very small portion and a very select segment of American society. Today, there are 1.4 million men and women on active duty in all four branches of the armed forces. The army and marines, which are bearing the brunt of the fighting, have only 700,000 people between them. This is in a country of over 300 million people. In 1968, at the height of the war in Vietnam, there were 3.4 million people in the armed forces out of a total population of about 200 million; in Korea it was 4 million in a nation of 150 million.

Moreover, this one-half of one percent of the population in today's armed forces comes mainly from rural areas and from families making less than $50,000 a year. Because there is no draft to spread the burden around, there are almost no individuals from the upper echelons of society serving in the armed forces. Paradoxically, the fact that the GWOT is being waged by such a small and limited portion of the populace has created feelings of guilt among the elite and has led to a groundswell of support for the returning veterans, something that did not happen during the war in Vietnam. In fact, veterans of that conflict were often treated as pariahs and some were accused of war crimes for carrying out their duties.

Ninth, the nature of the wars in Iraq and Afghanistan is markedly different from previous conflicts and much more challenging for the individual fighting person. Korea was a conventional war fought against the armies of North Korea and China. In Vietnam, the United States fought against the North Vietnamese regular army and the Viet Cong guerillas who shared the goal of creating a unified communist Vietnam. In Iraq, the United States is simultaneously fighting several groups, many of whom have different agendas and who often fight each other.

For example, tens of thousands of Sunni insurgents, who killed and wounded thousands of Americans from 2003 through 2006, have become the Sons of Iraq and allies of the United States. They are now being paid by the Iraqi government and trained by American soldiers and marines. Similarly, the U.S. military has often had to fight Shiite militias that support the American-backed government of Prime Minister Al-Maliki.

Consequently, it is difficult for the soldier or the marine on the ground in Iraq to tell friend from foe. This puts tremendous pressure on the troops to decide when and where to use lethal force. Moreover, the insurgents often hide among the civilian population. This has resulted in a significant number of innocent civilians being killed inadvertently by Americans during military operations and several soldiers and marines being prosecuted for battlefield crimes.

As a result of these nine unique factors, today's veterans are experiencing far more physical and especially mental problems upon their return from the war zone than veterans of previous wars. Divorces, suicide attempts, spousal abuse and sexual harassment are all skyrocketing as veterans return home from the wars in Iraq and Afghanistan.

In this volume, we will deal with the impact of these issues on today's veterans and the country. The sections below give a brief introduction to the following chapters.

To provide a historical context for today's challenges, Chapter 2 analyzes the question of how America has decided what it owes its veterans from the Revolutionary War to the present. Throughout American history, benefits for the nation's veterans have always been subject to political debate. Generally, politicians have been split into two camps—those who favor generous benefits based upon a sense of national obligation, and those whose primary concern has been the nation's balance sheets. All too often, fiscal conservatives have won out, forcing veterans to fight for benefits. While most Americans tend to assume that there is a broad consensus as to what the nation owes its veterans, history shows that this imagined consensus has rarely if ever existed.

It took roughly 40 years after the end of the Revolutionary War for Congress to provide a pension to indigent veterans of the Revolutionary War. But it was not until the Civil War that the government began to provide for its veterans in a systematic fashion. For political reasons, Congress repeatedly expanded post-Civil War benefits from a program to assist disabled veterans to a general old age pension for soldiers. The direct political benefits members of Congress derived from generous benefits for veterans outweighed concerns about fiscal responsibility.

After World War I, veterans were promised a bonus to make up for the low pay they received as soldiers prosecuting the war in comparison to civilians producing war matériel at home. To get the measure past fiscal conservatives, Congress delayed the bonus until 1945. But when the Great Depression struck in 1929, many veterans began demanding early payment of the bonus. A group of veterans known as the Bonus Expeditionary Force or Bonus Army actually marched on Washington, D.C., but were rebuffed by the Hoover administration and cleared out by the Army.

The poor treatment of World War I veterans remained in the minds of the Roosevelt administration and others in Congress as the nation prepared for World War II. Franklin Delano Roosevelt framed general principles for veterans benefits based upon the nation's obligation to its veterans, and Congress, working together with the American Legion, produced the most sweeping veterans benefit in American history: the GI Bill of Rights. The GI Bill assisted millions of veterans and helped build the fabled postwar middle class. It continues to provide the gold standard for veterans benefits to the present day.

Like World War I veterans, Vietnam veterans had to fight for their benefits. Confronted with new problems like posttraumatic stress disorder and

Agent Orange poisoning, Vietnam veterans themselves actually forced the government to acknowledge its responsibility to those it sent to war. Veterans spearheaded the drive for Vet Centers, where veterans could talk with other veterans about their adjustment problems. Lawsuits, congressional action, and an inquiry by retired Admiral Elmo Zumwalt, former chief of naval operations whose son died of Agent Orange, forced the Department of Veterans Affairs to acknowledge the serious side effects of the Agent Orange defoliant. It took nearly 20 years after the end of the war, but Vietnam veterans finally began to receive full benefits from their government.

The recent wars in Iraq have created a new generation of veterans. Many veterans of the First Gulf War have reported symptoms of a Gulf War syndrome, which has only recently been confirmed to exist by the VA. In contrast to historical precedent, Congress has acted swiftly to deliver benefits to veterans of the wars in Iraq and Afghanistan. The so-called 21st-century GI Bill, sponsored by Vietnam veteran Senators Jim Webb (D-VA) and Chuck Hagel (R-NE), provides generous education benefits not seen since the original World War II–era GI Bill to America's new veterans.

The treatment of our veterans is not just a question of political will and resources; it is also a question of organization. Analysis shows that even a generously funded program will not help veterans if it is not properly administered. Chapter 3 explores the position of the Department of Veterans Affairs within the U.S. government and American politics. This chapter argues that the political clout of veterans helps ensure the protection and continuation of the extensive benefits provided to veterans.

While social security has been described as the "third rail" of American politics—meaning that it is so politically popular that any effort to reform it would likely electrocute the reformer—the same can probably be said of the VA system. Over the last 30 years the Department of Veterans Affairs has survived relatively unscathed, and was perhaps even strengthened, in an era when the conservative vision of reducing the size of government dominated the political landscape. The elevation of the Veterans Administration to cabinet-level status occurred in 1988 during the Reagan administration. An administration that came into office pledging to eliminate government agencies closed its second term by adding a new one. In the mid 1990s, despite the Republican revolution—a movement that ushered massive conservative majorities into Congress on a pledge to balance the budget and decrease the size of government—the second largest government agency, which operates a government-run healthcare system and provides extensive benefits, was never a serious target for spending cuts. Unlike social security, few have argued for dramatically restructuring or overhauling the Department of Veterans Affairs.

Instead, the major political parties have engaged in an intense debate over who supports veterans and veterans benefits the most. Throughout each of the last four presidential campaigns, veterans benefits have become a prominent political topic. In each of these presidential elections each of the major party candidates have pledged to maintain or increase spending on veterans benefits.

The political clout of veterans groups helps explain much of the current support for the VA system. There are about 24 million veterans in the United States and about a quarter of the U.S. population, or roughly 61 million people—including veterans and their beneficiaries—are eligible for veterans benefits. Such a large benefit system has led to the development of a massive government bureaucracy. The Department of Veterans Administration is the second largest government agency behind the Department of Defense. It has an annual budget of roughly $70-$90 billion per year and employs 230,000 people at VA medical centers and offices around the country. The growth of the VA did not happen without significant political backing. There are a number of very strong civil society groups that support strengthening efforts to help veterans.

However, since the creation of the all-volunteer military in 1973, the overall veteran population is shrinking. Approximately 900 World War II veterans die every day and about 40 percent of all veterans are over the age of 65. Not only does caring for such a large aging population have considerable costs, but it might also have potentially adverse implications for the political clout of veterans as the population of veterans declines. Yet if anything the political influence of veterans seems to have grown over the last decade. Much of this is due to the wars in Afghanistan and Iraq, the politicization of patriotism, and the declining number of veterans serving in congress. Both Afghanistan and Iraq are the first protracted wars to be fought by an all-volunteer military, which has put tremendous strain on those who volunteered to serve. This has created an intense feeling of obligation throughout the country, and especially among those political leaders who have not served in the military, to demonstrate support for veterans, and this is usually done through supporting veterans benefits.

Nevertheless, the political clout of veterans has not meant that the Department of Veterans Affairs is without problems. While funding has increased, the VA system has been placed under tremendous strain by the protracted conflicts in Iraq and Afghanistan. In some respect, inefficiencies and poor management are an inherent trait of very large bureaucracies. But many of the problems in the VA are also reflective of a governing philosophy that holds government benefit and entitlement programs in disdain. While the Bush administration increased the budget of the Department of

Veterans Affairs somewhat, a government and agency that was managed and run by individuals who believed that government is often part of the problem frequently took a hands-off approach.

Chapter 4 outlines the demographics of the current veteran population—those veterans who have already separated from active or reserve service and fall under the jurisdiction of the Department of Veterans Affairs.

Public attention over the last seven years has understandably focused on the ability of the Department of Veterans Affairs to provide for the needs of the hundreds of thousands of Iraq and Afghanistan veterans currently entering the VA system. Less attention, however, has been paid to the agency's ability to care properly for the entire veteran population, including the millions of veterans from previous eras who are already in the system. Together, these two populations are placing an enormous amount of stress on the VA system-wide, a strain that is beginning to affect its ability to provide proper and timely care to all veterans seeking care.

In terms of demographics, the current veteran population—veterans of previous conflicts—in the United States is shrinking, but will require a great deal of specialized care over the long term. Today, there are over 24 million living veterans and an additional 37 million spouses, children, or other veteran dependents and survivors of deceased veterans. Together this population amounts to about 20 percent of the entire U.S. populace.

This chapter analyzes current trends within the active services—particularly the ground forces—that ensure that the Department of Veterans Affairs will be responsible for providing care for a large number of veterans with severe physical and mental injuries for years and decades to come. The chapter examines in detail the effect that several unique aspects of the wars in Iraq and Afghanistan have had on the number of veterans who will seek the health care and monetary benefits from the VA to which they are entitled. Specifically, Chapter 4 demonstrates:

- The actual number of physically injured military personnel from Iraq and Afghanistan is far higher than the number commonly reported by the Department of Defense;
- Today's prolonged and repeated deployment cycles significantly increase the risk of psychological injuries;
- Lengthy and repeated deployments in Iraq and Afghanistan have inflicted psychological and cognitive injuries on a large number of service members;
- The types of psychological injuries suffered by service members in Iraq and Afghanistan take months if not years to recognize; and
- High rates of service members are surviving battlefield injuries that would have been fatal in past conflicts.

Chapter 5 examines the issues impeding the quality care and benefits that can and should be provided to veterans returning from Iraq and Afghanistan. It answers the question of whether the veterans heath care system is up to the task of providing physical and mental care to the new veterans while simultaneously dealing with the needs of the millions of veterans from previous conflicts.

Given the laudable quality indicators discussed briefly in Chapter 5, the quality of care that veterans receive once in the VA health care system is not the main focus of this chapter. This is not to say that the VA health care system does not have its fair share of problems. Rather, the topic of this chapter is an analysis of the impediments veterans face in accessing that care.

Many of these impediments are the inevitable consequence of the sheer number of veterans seeking care discussed in Chapter 4. Put simply, today's volume exceeds the VA's capacity to provide for such a large number of veterans with diverse and complicated needs, and "the demand for VA medical treatment far outstrips supply."[8] Consequently, the VA has been forced to rely on its priority ranking system and waiting lists to regulate the number of veterans it can treat. Other impediments are the result of administrative hurdles inherent in the complicated process veterans must navigate in order to receive VA care.

Together, the increasingly large numbers of veterans demanding care and benefits from the VA and the administrative redundancies and inefficiencies built into the process of receiving VA care have greatly reduced the ability of veterans to access that care. These impediments are the focus of this chapter.

Chapter 6 examines the multiple mental health problems experienced by the veterans of the wars in Iraq and Afghanistan. Throughout American history, various labels have been attached to returning service members who experience mental health problems and depression resulting from the pressures of combat environments—the invisible wounds of war. Although different labels have been applied over the years, soldiers' heart in the Civil War, shell shock in World War I, and battle fatigue in World War II, all the terms essentially described the same condition. Yet, as discussed in Chapter 2, it was not until after the Vietnam War that a broad recognition of the symptoms and causes of what has become known as posttraumatic stress disorder (PTSD) became widely recognized.

And as discussed in Chapter 4, psychological disorders resulting from the extreme pressures and stressful environments of combat are hardly unique to the wars in Iraq and Afghanistan. However, several aspects of both wars—tough grinding counterinsurgency warfare, close urban combat, and repeated and lengthy deployments characterized by short dwell times between deployments—have all contributed to the wide-spread prevalence of PTSD in today's returning service members.

The growing acceptance and recognition of PTSD and its related effects within the military and in civilian society have also led to a dramatic increase in PTSD awareness and diagnosis. Whereas seeking help for PTSD-related symptoms was once grounds for ridicule, career stagnation, and in some cases actual punishment, the military has undertaken a concerted effort to reduce the stigma surrounding the disorder. While anecdotal evidence suggests that the stigma has hardly disappeared from military culture, today's environment is much more conducive to military people seeking help than it has been in previous wars.

PTSD, however, is only one of the signature injuries of the wars in Iraq and Afghanistan. Traumatic brain injuries (TBI), cognitive dysfunctions resulting from an extreme external force, are also increasingly common in today's returning service members. Just as the grueling environments of Iraq and Afghanistan magnify the effects of PTSD, the signature weapons of the wars in Iraq and Afghanistan—extremely high powered explosives and electrically formed penetrators—multiply the instances of TBI.

The concluding chapter discusses President Obama's Secretary of Veterans Affairs General Eric Shinseki, the challenges that confront him, and the advantages he has as VA Secretary.

Notes

1. CBS News, "U.S. Sends Wounded Troops Back to Iraq," January 19, 2008, http://www.cbsnews.com/stories/2008/01/19/national/main3731718.shtml.

2. Mark Benjamin, "The Army is Ordering Injured Troops to Go to Iraq," *Salon Magazine,* March 11, 2007, http://www.salon.com/news/2007/03/11/fort_benning/.

3. Ibid.

4. Mark Thompson, "America's Broken-Down Army," *Time,* April 5, 2007, http://www.time.com/time/nation/article/0,8599,1606888,00.html.

5. Ann Scott Tyson, "Possible Iraq Deployments Would Stretch Reserve Force," *Washington Post,* November 6, 2006.

6. Julia Preston, "U.S. Military will Offer a Path to Citizenship," *New York Times,* February 15, 2009.

7. "Report: Stop Loss to Continue Through '09," *Stars and Stripes,* October 28, 2009, http://www.stripes.com/article.asp?section=104&article=58436.

8. Joseph Stiglitz and Linda Bilmes, *The Three Trillion Dollar War: The True Cost of the Iraq Conflict* (New York: W. W. Norton, 2008), 81.

CHAPTER 2

The History of Veterans Affairs

Peter M. Juul

Somewhat surprisingly, from the Revolutionary War to the present day, the question of what America owes its veterans and their families has been a politically controversial subject. Some politicians who spent extravagant sums to send men and women into battle repeatedly turn around to argue that providing benefits to those who fought would constitute an undue fiscal burden on the treasury. Benefits proponents, on the other hand, felt that American veterans deserved compensation for their service, or as Theodore Roosevelt put it in 1903, "a man good enough to shed blood for his country is good enough to get a square deal afterward."[1] The story of America's treatment of its veterans is the story of the political contest between these two views.

Throughout American history, much to our shame as a nation, fiscal conservatives have generally won out over advocates of generous treatment of veterans. From the Revolution to World War I, veterans' benefits consisted largely of comparatively small cash payments in the form of pensions or bonuses. These disbursements were often made conditional on injuries incurred while in service or upon reaching old age. For its part, the U.S. government often ignored or deferred spelling out benefits to veterans until after a particular conflict ceased. Only during World War II did the government formulate a plan to reintegrate returning veterans into society. This foresight resulted in one of the most far-reaching pieces of social legislation in American history: the GI Bill of Rights. While the World War II example should have provided a template for assisting future veterans, Vietnam vets were forced to fight an uphill battle against an indifferent public and hostile government to claim their due.

America's historical treatment of its veterans runs counter to contemporary political rhetoric about American society's commitment to its warriors. More often, the country has treated its veterans, in the words of Vietnam vet William Crandell, like "expended brass...not even worth picking up."[2] While the post–World War II GI Bill is enshrined in the public memory, recognizing America's less than exemplary treatment of veterans of other wars serves to illustrate the fundamentally political nature of the veterans issue. Only by coming to grips with this historical truth can Americans fully examine the current state of veterans' issues and decide on how best to honor the current generation's service.

The First Veterans: From the Revolution to the War of 1812

From the very beginning of the Republic, the issue of veteran compensation was a major issue. Early in the Revolutionary War, officers in George Washington's Continental Army pressed for pensions worth half their service pay. Washington initially balked at their proposal, concerned about costs and popular reaction, but a wave of officer resignations (over 200 in total) in late 1777 and early 1778 prompted him to write to the president of Congress. Worried more about defeating the British and without the need to be concerned about future costs, Congress passed a half-pay pension for officers in early 1778 despite having no power to tax, and thus no way to pay. Another half-pay measure was passed but then rescinded the following year; Congress finally made up its mind on the matter in 1780 when it passed a measure granting half-pay to those officers who remained in the army for the duration.[3] Initially estimated to cost from $400,000 to $500,000—equal to the total revenues of the federal government at the time and between $6,250,000 and $7,600,000 in 2007 dollars—the cost of officers' pensions had increased so much by 1783 that officers were instead given certificates worth five years' pay.[4]

It would take decades and another war for the average minuteman to receive similar treatment. In December 1817, with the luxury of a then-considerable budget surplus of $2.7 million, President James Monroe proposed granting a pension to indigent veterans of both the Revolution and the recent War of 1812. Monroe justified such a pension by citing the debt "to the surviving officers and soldiers of our Revolutionary Army, who so eminently contributed, by their services" to the nation.[5] The subsequent debate over the pension in Congress would set the parameters for the debate about veterans benefits until World War II.

While Monroe framed his pension request in terms of what the nation owed its veterans, opponents of the measure emphasized its financial costs.

Some, like Representative (and future president) William Henry Harrison, argued that only veterans who had served more than six months should be included, while others, like Senator William Smith, contended that giving veterans pensions would be the first step down a slippery slope toward comprehensive aid to the nation's poor. For their part, supporters of aid to veterans, like Representative Joseph Bloomfield, seriously underestimated the total cost of Monroe's pension program. In the end, Monroe's program passed without a means test for poverty.[6] Officers would receive $20 a month, while enlisted soldiers would get $8 a month.[7]

In fact, the pension program—estimated by Bloomfield to cost only $500,000—wound up costing more than three million dollars.[8] More than 15,000 veterans received pensions as a result of Monroe's pension program;[9] however, the perceived need for government austerity following the Panic of 1819 led to dramatic retrenchment. In 1820, Congress stipulated that veterans needed to submit proof of poverty to receive a pension. Those veterans currently on pension rolls and whose poverty could not be determined were cut from the rolls; over 6,000 veterans lost their pensions during a period of national financial distress. The nation weathered the economic crisis, and by 1823, Congress passed legislation reinstating those veterans who had become victims of financial austerity.[10]

Over the next decade, pensions began to consume a greater and greater proportion of the nation's finances. In 1833, Congress chartered the Bureau of Pensions, the "the first administrative unit dedicated solely to the assistance of veterans,"[11] to manage veterans' pensions. By 1844—two years before the outbreak of the Mexican-American War—pensions accounted for 36.8 percent of the War Department's budget. After the war, financial responsibility for pensions was transferred to the Department of the Interior. Mexican-American War veterans would not receive their own $8 a month pension until 1887, nearly 40 years after the war.[12]

The Politics of Pensions: The Civil War and Its Aftermath

The Civil War was America's first democratic war; as sociologist Theda Skocpol notes, "the entire adult male citizenry was subject to calls to military service." Over 2.2 million men served in the Union armed forces—roughly 37 percent of the northern male population aged 15 to 44.[13] At war's end, the total number of American veterans jumped dramatically to 1.9 million.[14] As a result of the widespread nature of military service, Civil War veterans had the political clout to lobby for fair benefits from the nation they had served.

The first veterans benefits law relating to Civil War service was passed in February 1862. This law was closely related to the need to raise an army to put down the southern rebellion: prior to the advent of conscription in 1863, the Union army was dependent on volunteers to fill its ranks. To provide an incentive to volunteer, Congress awarded pensions to soldiers with disabilities caused directly or indirectly by injuries incurred on duty. These benefits were distributed according to rank; officers ranked lieutenant colonel and above who were injured in the line of duty would receive $30 a month, while a private with similar disabilities would receive only $8 a month (this was later revised in 1873 to pay by degree of disability). Later laws provided for special benefits for certain types of disablement, such as blindness or loss of both hands, which required specialized care. Under the initial pensions legislation, widows and dependents of soldiers who died as a result of their service became entitled to survivors' benefits at rates equal to "total disablement." While the 1862 law only provided benefits to one dependent, later legislation in 1873 granted additional benefits for dependent children.[15]

In addition to providing pensions, Congress also sought look after severely disabled veterans. Soldiers were entitled to either modest one-time cash payments ($50 for a missing arm or $75 for a missing leg) or a government-supplied artificial limb that could be replaced every three years.[16] Following President Abraham Lincoln's call "to care for him who shall have borne the battle and for his widow, and for his orphan," Congress created the National Asylum for Disabled Volunteer Soldiers, later known as the National Home for Disabled Volunteer Soldiers.[17] By 1870, branches had opened in Maine, Wisconsin, Ohio, and Virginia, and were caring for 3,200 disabled veterans.[18] Despite the support of Generals Ulysses S. Grant and George Meade and Admiral David Farragut, some public officials objected to the creation of disabled veterans' homes. Governor Alexander Hamilton Bullock of Massachusetts, for example, argued that soldiers' homes would simply siphon off money needed elsewhere.[19]

The fiscal cost of Civil War pensions was quite large. Before the Civil War, 10,700 veterans and widows received a total of roughly one million dollars; in 1866, one year after Lee's surrender to Grant at Appomattox, 126,722 veterans and widows were on the pension rolls, costing $15.5 million. As time went on and Congress liberalized pension laws, costs and pensioners steadily increased until leveling off in the mid-1890s. By the 50th anniversary of the war's start, pensions cost roughly $160 million a year.[20] This period of pension expansion serves to illustrate the central role of politics in determining the shape and nature of veterans benefits.

The first significant expansion of Civil War pension benefits occurred with the passage of the Arrears of Pension Act in January 1879. The Arrears Act, as it became known, allowed veterans who had been awarded pensions after the war to receive additional payments back to the date of their discharge from the military. New applicants (until July 1880) would receive a lump-sum payment of their arrears from the date of their discharge. Over 140,000 additional men were put on the pension rolls in the first year of the Arrears Act. Disabled vets received an average of $953.62, while widows and dependents got $1,021.51. Since the average annual earnings for nonfarm workers was $400, these payments amounted to nearly two and a half years' income to disabled veterans and widows. President Rutherford B. Hayes later pointed out in defense of the Arrears Act, "In every county of the North are small but comfortable homes built by the soldier out of his arrearage pay."[21]

But it was not out of simple gratitude or sense of obligation that Congress passed the Arrears Act. By the late 1870s, with the end of Reconstruction and the reintegration into national life of the heavily Democratic south, national politics entered a period of intense electoral competition. Hayes, a Republican, lost the popular vote in the 1876 election and entered the White House by virtue of a special congressional commission. Northern Democrats, eager to prove their patriotic bona fides, passed Arrears legislation in the Democratic-controlled House of Representatives before the Republican-controlled Senate could do so. As one northern Democrat stated, the House's swift action on the Arrears Act refuted "every accusation against the [D]emocratic party of want of regard for the interest of the soldier."[22]

The sheer number of new pension applicants as a result of the Arrears Act soon created a substantial backlog in the Bureau of Pensions. Many veterans turned to their elected representatives to rectify what they perceived to be injustices in pension distribution procedures. Famed progressive Senator Robert LaFollette of Wisconsin estimated that during his 1885–1891 service in Congress, he spent a quarter to a third of his time helping veterans obtain their pensions. During the 49th Congress of 1885–1887, 40 percent of House legislation and 55 percent of Senate legislation dealt with "special pension acts" designed to add individuals whose claims had been rejected by the Bureau of Pensions to government rolls.[23]

The Bureau of Pensions itself was not above politics. In the month preceding the national election of 1880, the number of pension claims it awarded increased by more than 150 percent over the previous three months. More egregious was the behavior of the Commissioner of Pensions, Colonel W. W. Dudley, who in 1884 directed officials to speed up claims-processing in the critical states of Ohio and Indiana in an effort to defeat Democratic candidate Grover Cleveland. Once in the White House, Cleveland moved away from the Democrats' earlier enthusiastic support for pensions, and stressed the need to control costs and reduce the tariff, then the nation's primary source of revenue. In the 1888 campaign,

Republicans made an issue of Cleveland's veto of the Dependent Pension Bill of 1887, a move to grant a pension to every Union veteran and his survivors. Their candidate, retired General Benjamin Harrison, owed his 1888 victory to the mobilization of veterans votes by the Grand Army of the Republic, the largest and most influential Civil War veterans' organization.[24]

Harrison made good on his political debt to Civil War veterans by getting Congress to pass the Dependent Pension Act of 1890. The new legislation eliminated the connection between war injuries and pensions; if a veteran was disabled for any reason at any time and had served at least 90 days during the Civil War, he or his dependents could receive a pension. Just as after the Arrears Act, pension expenditures dramatically increased. Three years after the Dependent Pension Act's passage, nearly a million people were on the government's pension rolls, accounting for 41.5 percent of the total national budget. While the pension issue receded in salience as the Republican Party solidified its political dominance at the turn of the century, it did not disappear completely. In 1906, Congress essentially converted the disability-based pension into an old age pension by deciding that the age of 62 was to be considered a disability for veterans.[25] Pension liberalization culminated with the Sherwood Act of 1912, which awarded old age pensions to all veterans of any conflict regardless of disability. The establishment of the post-Civil War pension system obviated the need for any new legislation in the wake of the Spanish-American War of 1898, the occupation of Philippines and the subsequent guerrilla war.[26]

Mobilizing for a Bonus: World War I Vets Fight for Benefits

As in the Civil War, America's intervention in World War I required the mass mobilization of the population. Roughly 4.7 million Americans, mostly conscripts, served in the armed forces during World War I. More than 116,000 were killed and an additional 204,000 wounded during the course of the war. The first benefit granted to these doughboys was a provision for government-subsidized life insurance through the War Risk Insurance Act Amendments of 1917. While voluntary and deducted from soldiers' pay, nearly 93 percent of those eligible took the insurance. Also incorporated into the 1917 amendments were provisions for rehabilitation and vocational training for permanently disabled veterans. Another law, the Vocational Rehabilitation Act of 1918, expanded similar benefits to all honorably discharged disabled veterans and granted cash allowances to those unable to work. All veterans were given $60—the equivalent of two months' pay—upon their discharge at the end of the war.[27]

Returning home from "over there," many veterans resented the fact that civilian pay had increased by 200 to 300 percent during the war while they subsisted on low levels of military pay, which remained stagnant. The newly formed American Legion began lobbying Congress to "readjust" servicemen's pay—to compensate veterans for the wages they gave up due to their service. While Congress acknowledged the legitimacy of the doughboys' grievance with the $60 mustering out pay, veterans organizations, led by the Veterans of Foreign Wars founded in 1899 after the Spanish-American War, began lobbying for additional compensation. No fewer than 75 bills providing for a "bonus" were introduced in Congress a year and a half after the armistice. Despite congressional enthusiasm for some form of compensation, the administration of President Woodrow Wilson was not eager to incur the expense. Secretary of the Treasury David F. Houston estimated a bonus would cost the taxpayers $2 billion; while the House ignored the administration's dire cost estimates and passed a bonus bill, the Senate heeded Wilson's concern for fiscal responsibility and let the bill die.[28]

Though lawmakers had for the moment tabled the bonus, in 1921 they consolidated the various veterans' programs and agencies under the newly created Veterans Bureau. Newly elected President Warren G. Harding appointed Colonel Charles R. Forbes as the bureau's first director. Unfortunately, the Veterans Bureau was beset with corruption and inefficiency. One subordinate agency, the Federal Bureau for Vocational Rehabilitation, was so inept that less than a quarter of eligible disabled veterans were enrolled in training, and 30 percent of those approved for training dropped out due to delays. During Forbes' tenure, the Veterans' Bureau processed only 47,000 claims for combat injuries—despite the fact that over 200,000 veterans were wounded during the war.[29] Forbes's incompetence as Veterans Bureau administrator was matched only by his corruption. By the time he resigned in February 1923, Forbes had bilked taxpayers out of $250 million, and was later convicted of conspiracy to defraud the government. His successor, retired Brigadier General Frank Hines, successfully reorganized the Bureau (re-designated the Veterans Administration in 1930), and as a result veterans expenditures rose 62 percent from 1924 to 1932.[30]

Throughout Forbes' trials and tribulations, Congress continued to consider the issue of veterans compensation. President Harding, who as a senator had enthusiastically supported the bonus, performed an about-face once in office. Claiming a bonus would increase the national debt, Harding and Secretary of the Treasury Andrew Mellon, who made cutting taxes a higher priority, directly intervened to prevent Congress from even considering a bonus for veterans. When Congress passed a bonus bill in 1922, Harding promptly vetoed it, claiming hypocritically that the nation did not have the money while at the same time advocating a tax cut. An attempted override of Harding's veto failed by four votes in the Senate. In the midst of coping with a series of scandals the next year, Harding died, leaving one of the most corrupt administrations in history as his primary legacy.[31]

Calvin Coolidge, Harding's successor, would prove no more amenable to a bonus when it was introduced in February 1924. Representative Hamilton Fish, Jr. introduced a measure that would have deferred payment of a bonus until 1945. Once again, Congress passed the measure and the president again vetoed it. Like Harding, Coolidge cited fiscal concerns as a primary reason for the veto, adding, "Patriotism which is bought and paid for is not patriotism." Angered by Coolidge's apparent insult to the over four million doughboys, Congress overrode the veto and mandated that "adjusted service compensation" would be paid, with interest, in 1945. Vets who served between April 5, 1917, and July 1, 1919, would receive compensation at a rate of $1.25 a day for overseas service and $1 a day for home front service. Over three million veterans received certificates worth three-and-a-half billion dollars, with an average per veteran payout of roughly $1,000. Despite the term "bonus," these certificates were in fact life insurance policies payable at death or in 1945. This unpleasant fact led to the program being given the morose nickname for the payment: the "Tombstone Bonus."[32]

When the Great Depression struck in 1929, many veterans were left with their bonus certificates as their only assets. In Congress, Representative Wright Patman became the leader of a coalition calling for immediate payment of the bonus. President Herbert Hoover rejected these calls, noting that two-thirds of the $900 million in spending on veterans was already going to World War I vets. In Hoover's mind, paying the bonus would require increased taxes and impede national economic recovery efforts. Despite the president's concern for the nation's balance sheets, pro-bonus forces insisted the nation should honor its commitments to its veterans. As Representative John J. Cochran, a Missouri Democrat, argued, the bonus "is not a dole, a handout; it is an adjustment in a very small degree of the soldier's pay while he served his country." Hoover was unsympathetic, and vetoed an immediate payment bill in February 1931. The day after Hoover's veto, Congress enacted legislation that allowed veterans to borrow up to half the final expected value of their bonus certificates.[33]

Despite congressional failure to act, veterans continued to agitate for immediate payment of the bonus. In Portland, Oregon, Walter W. Waters, a veteran who had participated in both World War I and the pre-war punitive expedition against Mexican revolutionary and outlaw Pancho Villa, concluded that veterans would have to go en masse to the nation's capital to lobby for immediate payment of the bonus. By mid-May 1932, after Congress killed any attempt to pay the bonus that year, Waters was able to convince enough veterans to set out for Washington, D.C., to push for the bonus. Assisted by sympathetic railroad workers, townspeople, and local and state officials, the "Bonus Expeditionary Force" (the BEF, a play on the American Expeditionary Force, or AEF, the official designation of the U.S. force deployed to France in 1917) made its way cross-country. Other veterans, inspired by news accounts of Waters' group, set out for Washington. By May 29, the first of Waters' BEF contingent arrived in the District.[34]

Pelham Glassford, the Washington police chief and a veteran of World War I, soon established an encampment for the BEF in the Anacostia neighborhood, across the river from Washington's Navy Yard. By June 8, 8,000 veterans marched to Capitol Hill, carrying placards scrawled with pro-bonus messages. Unique for its time, the BEF was integrated. As Roy Wilkins, then a reporter for the NAACP magazine *Crisis,* observed, "there was one absentee [at the BEF encampment], James Crow." In dramatizing the plight of indigent veterans, the BEF spurred Congress to reconsider Patman's tabled bonus payment legislation on June 14. Hoover's allies spoke out against the bill, emphasizing the need to maintain fiscal solvency. Proponents took the opposite position, arguing that the nation owed its veterans the bonus. As Representative James Frear stated, "They ask [for a bonus] from the wealthiest country in the world, for which they fought... They ask for bread, and Congress should not offer them a stone." While Patman's bill passed the House, it was defeated and tabled in the Senate. There would be no bonus in 1932.[35]

Despite this defeat, the BEF remained encamped in Washington. At the beginning of July, Glassford's police estimated some 21,100 veterans had descended on Washington to join the Bonus Army. One group of bonus marchers set up camp on Capitol Hill, marching in circles until Vice President Charles Curtis called 60 marines to "protect" the capitol building. Constant policing of BEF activities ground down Glassford's men. To President Hoover, the continued presence of the BEF was intolerable, and he informed the Washington, D.C., city commissioners that he wanted the veterans evicted.[36]

On July 28, Glassford's police moved to evict bonus marchers who were squatting in what is now Washington's Federal Triangle area. After a brief altercation at the Federal Triangle, vets from the main encampment in Anacostia began to stream into the center of the city. District commissioners, concerned that Waters could no longer control the BEF, decided to call in the army. By 2:30 that afternoon, troops under the watchful eye of army Chief of Staff General Douglas MacArthur had moved to the Ellipse, across from the White House. Shortly before that time, police attempting to evacuate a building shot two veterans, killing one and mortally wounding the other. At 4:30, MacArthur's troops set off to forcibly evict the BEF, marching down Pennsylvania Avenue. The troops tossed tear gas grenades to disperse the marchers, while cavalry—including a squadron under the command of Major George Patton—rode down veterans and locals who were simply observing the day's events. Soldiers burned down the makeshift structures housing the veterans and their families. For the first and only time in our history, army tanks rode through the streets of America's capital. Later that night, MacArthur's force cleared out the main BEF camp in Anacostia. The bonus march was over.[37]

But the bonus issue would not die. Congressional bonus advocates made another attempt to legislate the immediate payment of the bonus, led again by Wright Patman. But in May 1935, President Franklin D. Roosevelt, having swept Hoover out of office on the promise of "new deal" for the American people, personally delivered a veto message to Congress. After stating the usual fiscal rationale against immediate payment, FDR went to the nub of his argument: "Able-bodied veterans should be accorded no treatment different from that accorded to other citizens who did not wear a uniform during the World War." In FDR's view, the benefits the veterans were asking for should be guaranteed to all citizens. He instead advocated the passage of social security legislation to protect "all workers against the hazards of unemployment," including vets.[38]

Roosevelt's priority was fighting the depression. As he explained, "The veteran who is disabled owes his condition to the war. The healthy veteran who is unemployed owes his troubles to the depression." The House rejected Roosevelt's argument, but the president convinced enough people in the Senate to sustain his veto. Early in January 1936, however, the Congress overwhelmingly passed an immediate payment measure. Seeing the handwriting on the wall, FDR issued an obligatory veto that was promptly overridden in convincing fashion. World War I vets would receive government bonds $50 in worth, to be either held until 1945 or cashed in on June 15. An average veteran got $583 in bonus cash, which cost the government around $1.1 billion. The bonus payment wound up providing almost one percent of gross national product in economic stimulus.[39] As soon as World War I vets got their due, however, another global conflict lurked ominously on the horizon.

Avoiding the Mistakes of the Past: World War II and the GI Bill of Rights

In stark contrast to the way in which it entered all its previous American wars, the United States government made preparations for the return and reintegration of returning soldiers prior to entering World War II. The mechanism for the first small steps toward this goal was a provision of the Selective Training and Service Act of 1940, the first peacetime draft in American history. Section 8 of the act, the brainchild of Senator Elbert Thomas of Utah, required private and public employers to rehire employees who had been conscripted once they completed their service, provided they apply for reinstatement within 40 (later extended to 90) days after their discharge.[40] Such a requirement would avoid the situation faced by returning doughboys in 1918 and 1919, when many veterans found their prewar jobs occupied by others.[41] By the time President Roosevelt signed the act in mid-September, Britain had been at war with Nazi Germany for a year and the Chinese had been fighting Imperial Japan for over three years. It seemed only a matter of time before the United States would be dragged into the fighting.

Five days after the Japanese attack on Pearl Harbor finally brought America into the war, FDR ordered his aides to prepare a program for the reintegration of newly disabled veterans as productive members of society. Despite the president's early interest, bureaucratic gridlock prevented the formulation of legislation until the summer of 1942. FDR and his allies in Congress wanted a single Federal Rehabilitation Service to run job training for all disabled Americans, civilians and veterans. Opposition to the proposed legislation came from congressional conservatives, who viewed disabled veterans retraining as a stalking horse for New Deal–style reformism, and veterans groups like the American Legion, Veterans of Foreign Wars, and Disabled Veterans of America, who thought the proposal diluted the bureaucratic authority of the Veterans Administration. In the end, veterans groups won out and the legislation mandated that disabled veterans would receive exclusive treatment through the VA. Roosevelt promptly signed the measure in March 1943, which allowed veterans with 10 percent or greater disability and in service from December 6, 1943, onward (later liberalized by the GI Bill of Rights to the start of peacetime conscription in 1940) to receive up to four years of vocational rehabilitation.[42] Of the 670,000-plus veterans disabled in World War II, the VA was able to provide over 90 percent or 621,000 with job training.[43]

Looming even larger was the problem of demobilization. Once the war was won, what would become of the 16.1 million Americans who served in the armed forces?[44] Some legislators, like Vice President Henry Wallace, felt that something along the lines of a "Domestic Lend Lease" program would be necessary to avoid postwar economic collapse. In November 1940, FDR commissioned the National Resources Planning Board—a New Deal "alphabet soup" agency—to begin preparing for the postwar period. Even before Pearl Harbor, the NRPB had raised the question of whether or not demobilized vets should receive mustering out pay. Roosevelt approved full-scale planning in spring 1942, and the NRPB's Postwar Manpower Conference (PMC) met for the first time on July 17 of that year. The PMC met regularly to consider the problems of demobilization well into 1943.[45]

During the PMC's deliberations, several proposals were floated to facilitate the reintegration of servicemen and women into an economy in flux. Veterans Administrator Frank Hines favored holding service members beyond the duration of the war in order to reabsorb them gradually into the postwar economy. Colonel Frank Spaulding, the War Department representative, initially argued that vets should be given a three-month "furlough" in which to search for a job. If they found work, they would be released from service; if not, a veteran could return to the armed forces and receive military-run educational or training services. Others, such as NRPB executive director Charles W. Eliot, wanted the PMC to take a broader view of veterans readjustment, with an eye to expanding the program to the general population over time. This attitude led to a third proposal, in which veterans would be immediately discharged and post-service training and education made available to them. Unable to come to a consensus, the PMC asked FDR to break the deadlock; however, the president demurred and sent the issue back to the planners.[46]

The PMC produced a report by June 1943, shortly before the NRPB was decommissioned by congressional opponents of the New Deal. Their report urged that the government should concentrate its efforts to reintegrate returning veterans on employment. To achieve that goal, the PMC advocated that all veterans have the opportunity to obtain a year of training or education, along with a supplementary competitive federal scholarship program for those whose education had been interrupted. Educational programs would be tied to demand; no training would be provided for jobs for which the supply of labor was already plentiful. Despite the inability of the PMC report to gain political traction, the faint outlines of what would evolve into the GI Bill of Rights were visible in its proposals.[47]

While FDR had been noncommittal to the PMC's proposals, he did lay down a marker for postwar planning in his fireside chat of July 28, 1943. Referencing the post–World War I experience, FDR began the speech by informing the nation the government was laying plans for the return to civilian life for our gallant men and women in the armed services. They must not be demobilized into an environment of inflation and unemployment...We must, this time, have plans ready—instead of waiting to do a hasty, insufficient, and ill-considered job at the last moment.[48]

In that same speech, the president went on to establish priorities for legislative action: mustering-out pay and unemployment insurance for veterans unable to find work. His administration provided "An opportunity for members of the armed forces to get further education or trade training at the cost of the government," and comprehensive social insurance to include pensions and medical care. For the first time, Roosevelt came down firmly on the side of the nation's obligations to its veterans, concluding "the members of the armed forces have been compelled to make greater economic sacrifice and every other kind of sacrifice than the rest of us, and they are entitled to definite action to help take care of their special problems."[49]

While FDR and his administration looked toward a broader program, however skeletal, of postwar veterans readjustment by mid-1943, some members of Congress pressed for adjusted compensation similar to that belatedly granted World War I vets. Hines went so far as to have the VA prepare a draft bonus bill. With much of the government focused on the war effort and unable to cobble together comprehensive legislation, FDR called on Congress to approve mustering-out pay in an effort to head off bonus advocates. Congressional wrangling delayed passage of the legislation until February 1944; in its final form, veterans who served overseas would receive $300 of mustering-out pay, while those who served more than 60 days in the United States would receive $200 and those who served less than 60 days would receive $100.[50]

In October 1943, just prior to the legislative fracas over mustering-out pay, Roosevelt presented the administration's veterans education plan to Congress. Building on the work of the PMC, FDR proposed that all veterans who served honorably for six months since the start of the draft in 1940 be eligible for one year's equivalent of financial aid for education. A smaller group of veterans would be eligible for three years of grants and loans. In selling the plan, FDR emphasized both the benefits to the economy and the obligations of the nation toward its veterans. Senator Elbert Thomas, who earlier had worked for reemployment rights for drafted vets, introduced the administration's education proposal. A month later, FDR requested Congress add unemployment insurance to the package of veterans' benefits being assembled.[51]

At the same time, the American Legion was developing its own legislative proposal incorporating all the elements proposed by FDR into a single bill. While driven by a sincere interest in veterans welfare, the Legion no doubt wished to point to its successful legislative efforts when competing with other veterans organizations for members. The Legion had three central goals: centralizing benefits in the VA, ensuring World War II veterans received benefits at least equal to those of World War I veterans, and allowing veterans to resume their prewar lives with the least possible disruption. As it released its proposed legislation to the public in early January 1944, the Legion branded it "a bill of rights for G.I. Joe and G.I. Jane." The name stuck.[52]

The American Legion's unified proposal differed little from the administration's package, especially in the area of education. It extended the service time requirement to nine months, limited universal benefits to one year to those vets whose education had been disrupted by the war, and included a $50 or $75 a month subsistence allowance depending on marital status. The VA could choose certain veterans to receive three years' additional education. Aside from consolidating veterans' benefits proposals in a single bill, the greatest innovation in the Legion proposal was a title granting veterans loans for homes and farms subject to VA approval. In addition, the Legion's bill included year-long unemployment benefits that included an anti-union provision preventing returning vets from participating in strikes.[53]

Taking both the administration's and Legion's proposals as their baseline, legislators began to mark up the GI Bill. Substituting Senator Thomas' education proposal for the Legion's, the Senate Finance Committee extended education and training benefits to all veterans except those receiving a dishonorable discharge, regardless of whether they had been pursuing education prior to the war, while increasing the level of aid. Senator Robert Wagner of New York persuaded the Subcommittee on Veterans Legislation to liberalize the Legion's restrictive unemployment insurance disqualification measures. Following these revisions, the Senate approved the GI Bill unanimously. But trouble lay ahead in the House.[54]

Representative John Rankin, a conservative segregationist from Mississippi, chaired the Committee on World War Veterans' Legislation, the House committee through which the GI Bill had to pass. He vehemently disagreed with the education provisions of the Senate bill, proclaiming it would result in an "overeducated and undertrained" population. Rankin feared the unemployment compensation provisions even more, stating baldly that it would upset the prevailing racial caste system in the south by conferring benefits on black as well as white veterans. Despite Legion commander Warren G. Atherton's assertion that Rankin's comments were "an insult to the men in the service," after a brutal floor battle the House wound up passing a far more restrictive piece of veterans' legislation than the Senate.[55]

The two GI bills then proceeded to conference committee to hammer out the differences between the Senate and House versions. Rankin's obstructionism was defeated only by the creative intervention of the Legion, who arranged for an absentee Georgia representative to be flown in to vote in favor of the Senate version. With a workable compromise in hand, the bill returned to both chambers of Congress. Following their approval, Roosevelt formally signed the Servicemen's Readjustment Act on June 22, 1944.[56] In its final form, the GI Bill allowed veterans to collect $20 a week in unemployment compensation for up to a year, home and farm loans up to $2,000, and up to four years of education at $500 a year plus monthly subsistence payments of up to $120.[57] Amendments in December 1945 further liberalized the GI Bill, making it available to all veterans regardless of age or previous educational progress. Both subsistence benefits and the time window for using educational benefits were increased as well.[58]

The impact of the GI Bill on American society cannot be overestimated. When World War II vets' eligibility ended in the mid-1950s, 7,800,000 veterans—51 percent of all who served in the military—had taken advantage of the GI Bill's education provisions. Of these veterans, 2,200,000 went to colleges and universities while 5,600,000 obtained vocational training or other education. According to a 1998 survey of World War II veterans, 54 percent of those who attended college felt the GI Bill made college accessible. A whopping 77 percent of those who used the GI Bill for vocational training believed they would not have been able to afford training without government assistance. Over 50 percent of sub-college GI Bill users would not even have considered getting training without veterans' benefits. The bill's sub-college provisions were particularly helpful to less-educated veterans, who were two-and-a-half times more likely to use below-college benefits than similar veterans who attended colleges or universities. Those veterans who utilized sub-college benefits obtained a strong and near-immediate increase in occupational status and income, while those who used benefits to attend a college or university achieved increased status and income over time. Despite returning to a nation where Jim Crow unfortunately still held sway in some parts of the country, black veterans were just as likely as white veterans to take advantage of the GI Bill, though they were more likely to use sub-college provisions and less likely to use college benefits.[59] In a very direct way, the GI Bill helped create the broad middle-class prosperity of the postwar period through both its sub-college and higher education provisions.

While use of the GI Bill's loan guarantees was not as widespread as use of its education benefits, a significant number of veterans did take advantage of government backing to buy homes, farms, and businesses. Over a quarter of veterans—29 percent—used the guarantees, and of these veterans 93 percent bought homes, 5 percent businesses, and 2 percent farms. Despite government guarantees of up to 60 percent of each loan, the guarantee program was still susceptible to the whims and prejudices of lending agencies. Black vets in particular were severely hurt by discriminatory lending practices. Of 3,229 GI Bill loans in Mississippi, black veterans were granted just two.[60] In all, the loan guarantee program cost the government $50.1 billion.[61] Even fewer vets took advantage of the GI Bill's unemployment compensation provisions, an indication that the feared postwar depression did not materialize as expected. Veterans who did use unemployment benefits on average used less than 20 weeks of the 52 allotted, and only 14 percent used the full 52 weeks.[62]

As the war drew to a close in August 1945, changes were afoot at the Veterans Administration. Administrator Frank Hines struggled to cope with journalistic investigations of the VA's hospitals, and new President Harry S. Truman believed the VA needed to be "modernized." After all, the World War I veteran said, "I wouldn't have been happy to have the Spanish-American War veterans running the Veterans Administration, and I don't think the new veterans would. I think they would much rather have a general of their own war in the place." To achieve this goal, Truman replaced Hines with future five-star General Omar N. Bradley. While Bradley was unenthusiastic about leaving the Army to take the VA job, he brought a concern for the average vet to the VA. "We've got to look on veterans as individual problems, not as numbers in a file," he told his staff, "we must not forget that the service we give them they have earned by sweat and blood. It is a service they have paid for."[63]

Bradley nearly doubled the VA's field staff, and increased the central office staff by 5,000. By the time he left the VA in 1947, Bradley had overseen an unprecedented expansion.[64] He also got into a public spat with the American Legion when he moved to give hospitalization priority to veterans disabled by combat. Further, Bradley advised VA employees against membership in veterans organizations like the Legion, lest they show favoritism to its members. These moves were too much for Legion commander John Stelle, who, after failing to obtain a VA hospital for his hometown of Decatur, Illinois, demanded Bradley's resignation. Opposed by President Truman, General Dwight Eisenhower, other veterans' groups, the press, and even some Legionnaires, Stelle was forced to back down.[65] While it may have ruffled the Legion's feathers, Bradley's appointment reinvigorated the VA. As one historian put it, Bradley "changed the VA's image in a fortnight from a conservative agency serving World War I veterans to a dynamic organization more in harmony with its times."[66]

Despite minor bumps at the VA in the immediate postwar period, America's effort to assist its World War II veterans stands apart from all other attempts before or after. In particular, the GI Bill remains the gold standard for America's treatment of its veterans. Every major American war since World War II has seen a new iteration of the GI Bill passed. The first case was Korea, where Congress applied the same formula used to such success during World War II. Shortly after the war's start in June 1950, Congress passed legislation reactivating vocational training for disabled vets and extending benefits to peacetime veterans. In 1952, Congress passed the Korean GI Bill (formally known as the Veterans' Readjustment Act of 1952). While it incorporated nearly identical benefits to the World War II GI Bill, the Korean iteration offered smaller financial benefits and more restrictions than its World War II counterpart. Veterans were limited to 36 months of assistance at $110 a month, which was intended to cover both educational costs and subsistence.[67] Yet despite the generous example offered by the GI Bill in World War II and Korea, the veterans of America's next war would receive a distinctly different homecoming.

An Ungrateful Nation: Vietnam Vets Take On the System

At first, Vietnam veterans' benefits followed the script set by World War II and Korea. In early 1966—roughly a year after the first, large-scale deployment of American conventional ground forces to Vietnam—Congress passed the Veterans' Readjustment Benefits Act of 1966. Under its terms, any veteran who had been on active duty for 180 days or more was entitled to a monthly educational benefit of $100 a month for each month of service. The act went into effect on June 1, 1966, but applied retroactively to post–Korean War veterans.[68] But as more and more veterans returned from tours in a war becoming more and more unpopular, it became clear, to the vets at least, that the existing system for reintegrating veterans did not function for those it purported to serve. The Vietnam GI Bill was one, but only one, example: while 76 percent of eligible veterans participated, the program's educational benefit was nowhere near as comprehensive as its predecessors. Making matters worse, the inflation many vets faced upon returning to the United States in the early 1970s ate away at the benefits they did receive.[69]

Moreover, thanks to the lobbying of the American Legion, VFW, and other veterans groups, the VA hospital system was "tailor-made to serve the needs of the previous generation of veterans."[70] Only 10 percent of available hospital beds were occupied by Vietnam veterans, with the rest taken up by older veterans with non-service related injuries.[71] Senator Alan Cranston of California, after hearing complaints from Vietnam veterans in Los Angeles, toured VA hospitals and found them unresponsive to the needs of Vietnam vets. In December 1969, his subcommittee of the Senate Committee on Labor and Public Welfare heard the testimony of Vietnam veteran Max Cleland, a triple amputee and future VA head and United States senator from Georgia. Cleland told the assembled senators that the VA's medical procedures lagged behind the cutting-edge techniques that the military used to save his life: "When the severely disabled return from Vietnam, they face a rehabilitation process that is often based on World War II and Korean experience."[72] Making matters worse, VA hospitals were understaffed and as a result even severely wounded veterans were neglected; in some hospitals, such as the notorious Bronx VA that housed disabled veterans like Ron Kovic and Bobby Muller, later leaders of the Vietnam veterans' movement, rats and filth created unsanitary conditions.[73]

At the same time, a spotlight started shining on the psychological trauma suffered by many Vietnam vets. A loose network of people, some working in the VA and others with Vietnam Veterans Against the War, began noticing that veterans often returned with profound psychological problems. For example, in her first morning of work at the Boston VA hospital in September 1969, Sarah Haley encountered an emotionally agitated and anxious Vietnam veteran who told her of his experience in My Lai. While Haley took the vet's story of the infamous massacre at face value, the hospital's psychiatric staff dismissed it and classified the vet as a paranoid schizophrenic. Further experience with Vietnam veterans suffering from post-combat psychological problems convinced Haley the VA was drastically failing its obligations toward these new veterans. Since psychiatric manuals did not recognize post-combat stress as a psychological ailment, VA psychiatric workers were shunting vets with post-combat stress into established diagnostic categories. Because of this classification system, many vets with combat-related psychological problems were denied benefits by the VA because they could not trace their psychic injuries directly to combat. In 1974, Haley published an academic article arguing that veterans suffering from post-combat stress needed treatment drastically different than that traditionally dispensed by the psychiatric profession.[74]

At the same time, psychiatrists Robert Lifton and Chaim Shatan came to similar conclusions working with small, organic New York "rap groups" organized by Vietnam Veterans Against the War. In these groups, veterans would "rap" about their traumatic combat experiences. Informally observing the rap groups, Lifton and Shatan came to the conclusion that psychologically disturbed veterans suffered from "Post-Vietnam Syndrome."[75] At the same time, an unorthodox veteran named Shad Meshad was working on similar problems in Los Angeles. Knowing that he and his staff were not providing adequate care for Vietnam vets, Dr. Phillip May, director of psychological services at the Brentwood VA, hired Meshad to report on Vietnam veterans' special needs. Meshad argued that Vietnam vets needed to articulate and come to terms with their combat experiences rather than go through conventional therapy. To accomplish this objective, Meshad formed the Vietnam Veteran Resocialization Unit in the basement of the Brentwood VA. Feeling that most Vietnam vets would not come to a VA facility, Meshad pioneered community-based "storefront" counseling services to assist veterans.[76] Despite a growing awareness of the problem of post-combat psychological stress, it would be 1978 before the American Psychiatric Association officially recognized posttraumatic stress disorder (PTSD) as a legitimate psychological problem caused by combat.[77]

Concern for Vietnam vets' mental well-being extended into Congress, where efforts to improve the government's responsiveness to issues like PTSD ran into political walls. Senator Cranston, who had become chairman of the newly-created Veterans' Affairs Committee, introduced legislation in the spring of 1971 providing "readjustment counseling" as well as alcohol and drug treatment to returning Vietnam vets. While Cranston's proposal passed the Senate, it died in the House. There, the VFW and American Legion lobbied against Cranston's measure because these organizations feared it would take away funds from the older veterans who composed the vast majority of their membership. As Senator Max Cleland later remarked, the American Legion and VFW "gave great lip service to Vietnam veterans...But when it came time to funding programs for [Vietnam vets], boy, they thought it was going to take away from them. And they...fought tooth and nail, mostly quietly behind the scenes, to gut" legislation to help Vietnam veterans. Making matters worse, many members on the House Veterans Affairs Committee dismissed the idea that Vietnam veterans had special counseling needs.[78] Cranston would submit his bill no fewer than five times throughout the 1970s, only to see it repeatedly fail in the House.[79]

President Richard Nixon, a World War II veteran, was even less sympathetic to Vietnam veterans than the House of Representatives. While posturing as a friend of veterans, Nixon had his proxies telling Congress that Vietnam vets were "better off than World War II veterans." Donald Johnson,

Nixon's VA administrator, actually lobbied Congress to cut the VA's budget. When an unlikely coalition of senators—including recently defeated presidential candidate George McGovern and Nixon stalwart Bob Dole—crafted a generous new education benefit for Vietnam-era vets, the VA's benefits director warned the increases they had proposed would be "inflationary." These claims of economic ruin came at a time when Nixon had successfully wrung $600 million from a skeptical Congress to prop up South Vietnamese President Nguyen Van Thieu and was seeking nearly $3 billion more to keep his autocratic regime in power. In opposing McGovern and Dole's $250 million vet education program, Nixon revealed his own priorities: he would continue to fund the war, but not those who fought it.[80]

With Congress unable or unwilling to provide assistance, several activist Vietnam vets took matters into their own hands. In February 1974, a group of disabled veterans led by Ron Kovic, the activist of *Born on the Fourth of July* fame, staged a hunger strike in the California offices of Senator Cranston to protest hospital conditions and demanded a meeting with VA director Johnson. While they were able to get an audience with Johnson, who flew in to meet with the hunger strikers, Kovic's effort to organize a second bonus march out of the strike fizzled. Like President Nixon, Johnson would soon be forced to leave his office under a cloud of corruption. President Gerald Ford wound up appointing Johnson's successor, a World War II veteran and former VFW national commander named Richard L. Roudebush, to head the VA.[81]

The new director did not endear himself to Vietnam veterans either, calling them "crybabies." Jack Smith, a Vietnam veteran and PTSD activist then earning his psychology degree from Columbia University, made a proposal for a wide-ranging psychological study of Vietnam veterans; the government, fearful of the costs of providing treatment for PTSD, forbade the use of its funds to finance the project. Enraged by Roudebush's "crybabies" remark, Smith and several other vets hatched a plan to hold the VA administrator hostage in order to press their case. Using two-by-fours and nails, Smith and four others nailed themselves into an office with Roudebush in the VA's central offices in Washington. Unfortunately for Smith and his posse, Roudebush was encamped in the deputy administrator's office because his own office was being redecorated. The walls on which they attempted to nail the two-by-fours were cheap and easy to breach. Four hours after presenting their demands for a presidential commission on Vietnam veterans to Roudebush, guards broke in and arrested Smith and the others. Smith's imprisonment did not last long; since he had become something of a celebrity among other jailed vets, the Washington city jail released him to prevent further unrest.[82] Despite its failure, Smith's protest showed the lengths to which Vietnam veterans were prepared to go to ensure their legitimate issues were addressed.

Prospects for improvement seemed brighter when Jimmy Carter became president in 1977 and appointed triple-amputee Vietnam veteran Max Cleland to head the VA. Like the appointment of General Omar Bradley following World War II, Cleland's appointment marked a generational shift in the VA; many of his closest advisors had themselves served in Vietnam. Making readjustment assistance for Vietnam veterans a priority, Cleland's top aides met with Shad Meshad and other PTSD workers and advocates to formulate a program to deal with this "new" condition. He pushed Carter to establish a presidential review commission on Vietnam veterans, which wound up endorsing a specialized readjustment program. By 1978, the stars finally seemed to be aligning for Vietnam veterans to get readjustment assistance. The psychiatry establishment had at last accepted PSTD as legitimate, the president and VA administrator were more than sympathetic, and the first official caucus of Vietnam-era veterans formed in Congress.[83]

That year, Senator Cranston once again introduced his readjustment bill in the Senate, where once again it passed. Once again, it was held up in the House, where Veterans Affairs Chairman Ray Roberts of Texas wanted to shift the power to select the sites for new VA hospitals out of the executive and into his own committee. Senator Cranston and President Carter agreed on an arrangement by which Congressman Roberts would get his authority in exchange for the passage of the readjustment bill. However, Senator Warren Magnuson of Washington, chairman of the Senate Appropriations Committee, refused to share hospital construction authorization power with the Veterans Affairs Committees. This intrigue and intransigence delayed the passage of Cranston's readjustment legislation another year. Finally, more than six years after Richard Nixon signed the agreement ending American involvement in Vietnam, President Carter signed the Vietnam Veterans' Psychological Readjustment Act into law on July 13, 1979. This law marked the first major legislative victory for Vietnam veterans.[84]

The law established the Vietnam Veterans' Outreach Program, which would establish 137 storefront assistance locations, known as "Vet Centers," by 1981. Modeled on Shad Meshad's experiences in Los Angeles, these Vet Centers offered community-based readjustment counseling. Each Vet Center was to be staffed by three or four trained "paraprofessionals" who would help veterans cope with their psychological difficulties and inform them of their other veterans benefits. Looking back, Max Cleland stated that the Vet Center program was "the thing that I'm proudest of" as VA administrator.[85] Despite the fact that Vet Centers were to become one of the VA's most successful programs—with 232 centers serving all combat veterans across the United States in 2008[86]—they soon came under attack when a new administration came to power in Washington.

The advent of Ronald Reagan's administration in 1981 represented a shift back toward cost containment as the government's primary strategy in dealing with this nation's veterans. As part of an effort to cut nondefense discretionary spending to pay for the new president's tax cuts and massive military build-up, Reagan's budget director David Stockman planned to cut $900 million from the VA's budget. Stockman targeted the Vet Center program, even with its comparatively small $32 million budget, for termination. At a time when Reagan proposed the largest peacetime increase in military spending, these cuts were particularly galling to veterans and their supporters. Alan Cranston publicly chastised the Reagan administration, calling Stockman's plan "enormously insensitive and ill-advised." He pointed out that "our obligation to veterans is fundamentally a national responsibility...veterans programs are an inseparable cost of national defense." Cranston was even forced to sue Stockman to make the administration spend money Congress had already appropriated for the Vet Centers.[87] With the program in budgetary peril, Congress reauthorized the Vet Centers for another two years in June 1981; Congress would continue to protect the program as it established itself during the 1980s.[88] Future Nebraska Senator Chuck Hagel, a Vietnam veteran, resigned his number two post at the VA to protest Director Robert Nimmo's cavalier and inappropriate dismissal of Vietnam veterans' concerns.

At the same time that Congress and the Carter administration were focused on passing legislation establishing the Vet Center program, another Vietnam veteran issue began to surface: Agent Orange. From1962 to 1971, the United States conducted a massive aerial defoliation campaign throughout South Vietnam designed to destroy crops and deny the Viet Cong the cover of the jungle. In 1965, the Air Force switched from Agent Purple to the similar but less expensive Agent Orange; over the next six years, the Air Force sprayed nearly 11 million gallons of Agent Orange over South Vietnam. Production of one of the herbicides' major chemical components, a compound known as 2,4,5-T, also created dioxin.[89] At levels as low as five parts per trillion, dioxin is believed to cause cancer in certain laboratory animals; the least contaminated 2,4,5-T used in Agent Orange had dioxin concentrations considerably higher at one-tenth parts per million.[90]

As early as 1969, the Defense Department had become aware of the potential health dangers associated with Agent Orange. A National Cancer Institute study indicated trace exposure to dioxin caused cancer and birth defects in laboratory animals; in addition, South Vietnamese officials began reporting birth defects and a number of health issues in areas sprayed with Agent Orange. At this point, the military restricted defoliation to "remote" areas, and Secretary of Defense Melvin Laird dramatically slashed the budget for herbicide procurement by nearly 90 percent from $27 million to $3 million. Soon thereafter, the Pentagon temporarily banned Agent Orange from defoliation missions; this ban became permanent in January 1971.[91] In 1979, the Environmental Protection Agency issued a widespread ban on the use of herbicides containing 2,4,5-T.[92] In the government's eyes, it was clear that Agent Orange and its constituent chemicals posed a clear health risk.

By 1977, the VA began to receive claims from Vietnam veterans connecting their illnesses and disabilities to the use of Agent Orange. At the Chicago VA, a caseworker named Maude DeVictor received the case of Air Force veteran Charlie Owens. A pilot on the Agent Orange spraying missions, Owens had come down with terminal lung cancer and would die less than a month after being diagnosed. After Owens' spouse told her that the couple believed Agent Orange caused his cancer, DeVictor began looking for a connection between the herbicide and veterans' health problems. After making inquiries of Dow Chemical, the VA Central Office in Washington, the Department of Defense, and knowledgeable scientists, her supervisor told her to cease her investigation. By this point, however, DeVictor had assembled files on two dozen veterans exposed to Agent Orange, which she gave to local television reporter Bill Kurtis. In March 1978, Kurtis' CBS station broadcast a documentary entitled *Agent Orange: Vietnam's Deadly Fog*. Soon thereafter, the Chicago VA was deluged with veterans seeking information and treatment. To bring attention to this tragic situation, Representative Abner Mikva, a Chicago congressman, played Kurtis' documentary before the House Veterans Affairs Committee.[93]

Despite growing concerns of a relationship between Agent Orange and veterans' later health problems, rather than seek answers the Veterans Administration looked to head off claims. Coming at a time when he was fighting for PTSD assistance, the last thing VA administrator Max Cleland also needed was a drive for Agent Orange compensation.[94] Thus the VA's initial response was a May 1978 memo that told VA workers to inform veterans concerned about Agent Orange's effects that these effects were short-term and fully reversible. Two months later, the VA held a closed door meeting with a high-ranking medical representative of Dow Chemical and the former scientific director of the Air Force. These officials told the VA not to worry, that despite the EPA's objections, dioxin was not a contributor to anything worse than chloracne. By December, the VA created a Steering Committee on the Health Related Effects of Herbicides to articulate VA policy on Agent Orange disability claims. The committee concluded that since potential Agent Orange–related illnesses were not reported by veterans while on active duty or less than a year after veterans' discharges, they were not service connected and therefore not the VA's responsibility. The VA even went as far as telling its employees to discourage veterans from getting examinations for possible Agent Orange-related symptoms.[95]

As has been the case over and over, Vietnam veterans would once again have to agitate to get answers and action from the government. After reading of Maude DeVictor's account and her evidence of a connection between Agent Orange and various ailments, Paul Reutershan filed a claim with the VA over his stomach and liver cancer. Reutershan had been a helicopter crew chief in Vietnam, and often flew through misty clouds of Agent Orange. In addition to cancer, Reutershan's doctors diagnosed him with chloracne, an indicator of dioxin exposure. Replying to his claim, the VA said Agent Orange was not the cause of his cancer and even denied him treatment of his chloracne. Upset and unable to sue the government because of the legal doctrine of sovereign immunity, Reutershan instead filed a $10 million lawsuit against Dow Chemical and other Agent Orange manufacturers. Before his death in December 1978, Reutershan founded Agent Orange Victims International to carry on the fight for recognition and appropriate compensation.[96]

To the dismay of many veterans, the lawsuit would eventually be settled out of court in 1984. While the chemical companies paid $180 million into a trust fund, what the veterans really desired was recognition of Agent Orange's effects. The chemical companies explicitly denied liability for harm caused by Agent Orange in the settlement, despite documents discovered during the course of the suit that they were aware of dioxin's health issues as early as 1965.[97] Without an admission that Agent Orange could cause health problems, the VA could continue stalling on benefits for Agent Orange victims. However, the combined weight of the lawsuit, press reports, and other Vietnam veterans' protest (including a Ron Kovic–led takeover of the Wadsworth VA hospital in Los Angeles) enabled their supporters in Congress to get the legislative ball rolling as the 1970s gave way to the 1980s. Nevertheless, it would be almost a decade before the VA would recognize Agent Orange–connected disabilities as service-related and therefore deserving of benefits.

Congress held its first hearings on Agent Orange in June 1979. The House Subcommittee on Oversight and Investigation of the Committee on Interstate and Foreign Commerce heard testimony from Bobby Muller, the head of Vietnam Veterans of America, and Michael Ryan, a vet whose eight-year-old daughter Kerry suffered severe birth defects as a result of her father's Agent Orange exposure. Images of the wheelchair-bound Kerry created deep reservoirs of sympathy for Agent Orange victims. Shortly after these emotional hearings, Democratic Representatives Tom Daschle of South Dakota and David Bonior of Michigan, both members of the Vietnam-era veterans' caucus, introduced the first legislation forcing the VA to address the Agent Orange issue and compensate victims of the herbicide. Fellow caucus member Senator John Heinz, a Republican from Pennsylvania, pushed the legislation through the Senate, but once again Vietnam veterans' assistance legislation died in the House. Despite this failure, Congress did that year mandate the VA undertake an epidemiological study of the possible health effects of Agent Orange on veterans.[98] At the same time, the Carter White House formed the Agent Orange Working Group to coordinate the executive branch's response.[99]

Inexplicably, the VA dragged its feet and did not start the study for several years. Nearly three years after the study was authorized, Representative Daschle publicly accused "certain parties in the VA" of "deliberately trying to delay the Agent Orange study." In October 1982, President Reagan's hapless VA administrator, Robert Nimmo, punted responsibility for the study to the Centers for Disease Control.[100] At the same time, the General Accounting Office (GAO, today known as the Government Accountability Office) released a report damning the VA's response to Agent Orange. According to the GAO, the VA failed to provide adequate exams to veterans worried about Agent Orange exposure, and the computer database set up to track these cases was "inaccurate and unreliable." Moreover, the VA's director of environmental medicine admitted in congressional testimony that VA doctors were unaware of the symptoms of Agent Orange exposure.[101]

Throughout the 1980s, the VA's position was that a definitive link between Agent Orange and the medical problems had to be proven conclusively before veterans could be compensated. Veterans and their congressional advocates argued that the VA should presume a connection unless further evidence proved otherwise; this way, veterans would not suffer or die while waiting for research to come in. In late 1982, Representative Tom Daschle sponsored a bill granting a temporary presumption of a service connection between—and therefore compensation for— Agent Orange and the diseases chloracne, porphyria cutanea tarda, and soft-tissue cancers. All veterans suffering from these ailments needed to do was show they served in an area sprayed with Agent Orange. By March 1983, the Daschle bill had the support of 106 additional representatives and the VFW and American Legion, which both finally realized their organizational survival depended on recruiting Vietnam veterans. The VA opposed the bill, claiming Daschle's proposed compensation program would jeopardize the VA's finances. While the Agent Orange compensation bill passed the House, it failed in the Senate.[102]

Undeterred, Daschle would not give up his efforts to assist Agent Orange vets. In 1984, he would push through Congress the Veterans' Dioxin and Radiation Exposure Act that required the VA to set guidelines for Agent Orange compensation. Elected to the Senate in 1986, he cosponsored the Veterans' Agent Orange Disabilities Act of 1987 with highly decorated fellow Vietnam veteran Senator John Kerry, Democrat from Massachusetts. The Kerry-Daschle bill forced the VA to treat incidences of non-Hodgkins lymphoma, lung cancer, and immunosuppressive diseases believed caused by dioxin exposure as service-related for Vietnam veterans. Again, Daschle's presumption legislation passed in one house of Congress only to fail in the other. Holding up the Kerry-Daschle legislation was Representative and World War II veteran "Sonny" Montgomery of Mississippi, chairman of the veterans committee, who took the VA line that more studies were necessary to establish a relationship between Agent Orange and these diseases.[103]

It was not until 1987 that the final results of the CDC's Agent Orange study emerged. In August of that year, the CDC announced it canceled the study, saying it could not find any reliable data on which to base conclusions.[104] While the CDC was having methodological problems, a study commissioned by the American Legion in 1983 faced no such problems. Released on Veterans Day in 1988, the Legion study found that veterans exposed to Agent Orange and other herbicides had higher rates of skin conditions, benign tumors, and other problems. Miscarriages by spouses of exposed vets were roughly similar to those found in mothers whose spouses smoked during pregnancy. (The study also reinforced the link between PTSD and subsequent physical and mental health problems.) Concurrently, a U.S. District Court unsealed documents from the previously settled Agent Orange lawsuit indicating the military was at least partially aware of the herbicide's health risks as early as 1962.[105]

The emergence of this new information was the first crack in the VA's case against Agent Orange compensation. Over the next few years, the dam would burst. In 1989, President George H. W. Bush appointed former congressman Edward Derwinski as head of the Department of

Veterans Affairs (DVA), which had been elevated to cabinet status as a department at the end of the second Reagan administration. Derwinski told Congress he had "an open mind" on Agent Orange. Then, on May 3, Judge Thelton Henderson of the Northern District of California, ruling on a suit filed by the Vietnam Veterans of America against the VA, found the VA was failing to live up to the terms of the 1984 Dioxin Act. He therefore ordered the VA to reconsider 31,000 Agent Orange cases after drawing up new rules that abided by the Dioxin Act. Rather than appeal Henderson's ruling, Derwinski announced the DVA would comply and rewrite its regulations. To that end, the VA secretary appointed retired Admiral Elmo Zumwalt, Jr., the former Chief of Naval Operations, to look into the DVA's Agent Orange policies.[106]

Zumwalt, who had commanded the Navy's "brown-water" forces in Vietnam at the height of American involvement before becoming Chief of Naval Operations in 1970, had a personal connection to the Agent Orange issue. His son, Elmo III, had served under his command as a Swift Boat captain when the elder Zumwalt ordered defoliation to protect his crews. Elmo III's son, Russell, suffered from severe learning disabilities, and in 1983 Elmo III developed both non-Hodgkin's lymphoma and Hodgkin's disease. After studying the available literature, Zumwalt's son became convinced Agent Orange was responsible for his cancers. He died in 1988, a year before his father began investigating the VA's response to Agent Orange.[107] Assisted by a five-person team of medical experts and epidemiologists, Zumwalt discovered military and chemical company studies of dioxin exposure were conducted "fraudulently." When studies came close to ascertaining a link between Agent Orange and certain diseases, Zumwalt noted, "doctors who were associated with corporations in one way or another would maneuver the consensus away from a positive finding to an indeterminate finding...The scientists who went through the documents with me strongly agreed and came out infuriated at the pseudoscience that that represented." On May 5, 1990, Zumwalt concluded the U.S. government had, to its enduring shame, engaged in a "systematic effort to suppress critical data or alter results to meet preconceived notions of what alleged scientific studies were meant to find." He therefore asked Derwinski to "resolve doubts [about an Agent Orange-disease link] in favor of the Vietnam veteran."[108]

Shortly after Zumwalt issued his report, Derwinski announced the Department of Veterans Affairs would now presume a service connection between soft-tissue cancers and Agent Orange. Two months earlier, he had given presumption to non-Hodgkin's lymphoma. While Daschle proclaimed the DVA's decision "a major victory—one that Vietnam veterans have awaited for a long time," he was soon back to work on more Agent Orange legislation.[109] His new bill codified a new standard for judging Agent Orange claims: in addition to ratifying Derwinski's lymphoma and cancer decisions, Daschle's legislation set in stone the principle of giving veterans the benefit of the doubt on their herbicide claims. Despite this new evidence, Congress passed the new bill in 1991 only when confronted with the possibility American troops could be attacked with chemical weapons by Iraqi dictator Saddam Hussein when the United States led a coalition to evict the tyrant's forces from Kuwait.[110]

Throughout the 1990s, more diseases and conditions would be added to the list of presumptive links with Agent Orange exposure. By 1996, Vietnam veterans became eligible for compensation for Hodgkin's disease, porphyria cutanea tarda, prostate cancer, and peripheral neuropathy. In addition, that same year President Bill Clinton backed legislation for children of Vietnam veterans with spinal bifida to receive compensation from the VA—the first government extension of benefits to second-generation victims of Agent Orange.[111]

It had taken decades, but the United States had finally begun to live up to its obligations to veterans of the decade-long conflict in Southeast Asia. Moreover, Vietnam veterans established precedents and programs of which later veterans could take advantage. Vet Centers are now open to all combat veterans seeking counseling or other assistance. The battle for Agent Orange compensation helped spur early awareness of an emerging Gulf War Illness—a multisymptom condition that was believed to be connected to exposure to neurotoxins during the First Gulf War of 1991.[112] In 1994, Congress established the principle of presumption of service connection for veterans of the first Gulf War with undiagnosed illnesses and chronic disabilities. Congress expanded presumptive service recognition for Gulf War vets with fibromyalgia, chronic fatigue syndrome, and irritable bowel syndrome—three conditions associated with Gulf War Illness—in 2001.[113] While recognition of Gulf War Illness has certainly been faster than the recognition of Agent Orange-related illnesses, it has not always proceeded with alacrity. A recent study conducted by a VA special committee concluded that Gulf War Illness "is a real condition with real causes and consequences for affected veterans." It identified two major possible causes—pyridostigmine bromide, an anti-nerve agent drug, and pesticides used during the war—and advocated raising funding for research into Gulf War Illness to $60 million a year.[114] Nevertheless, the government response to recent veterans has been far superior to the treatment accorded Vietnam veterans.

The Evolution of the GI Bill

As noted, the World War II GI Bill is a touchstone for contemporary veterans policy. For every major postwar conflict the United States has entered, Congress has passed a new GI Bill. The first such effort was the Korean GI Bill, which passed in 1952. While this GI Bill was largely similar to its predecessor, its benefits were reduced and consolidated into a single monthly payment intended to cover both tuition and living expenses. The 1966 Vietnam GI Bill was initially intended to be even less generous, but as more and more veterans returned home and took advantage of education benefits monthly payments rose from an initial $100 a month to a high of $376 a month. Thanks to these mid-1970s increases, Vietnam GI Bill benefits eventually approached those of the original World War II GI Bill when measured in real dollars.[115] However, a combination of rapidly escalating education costs in the tuition of both private and public institutions and high levels of inflation in the 1970s and early 1980s eroded the actual value of Vietnam-era benefits. Further congressional efforts to increase benefit levels were either stymied by executive opposition or emasculated by recalcitrant committee chairmen.[116]

The World War II, Korean War, and Vietnam-era GI bills covered military forces largely composed of draftees. Benefits were justified on the basis that average citizens had been uprooted against their wishes from their civilian lives through conscription into military service; moreover, during their time in the military, draftees were paid only subsistence wages. Therefore the nation owed them assistance in returning to civilian life. However, after Vietnam the U.S. military switched from a conscription-based manpower base to an all-volunteer force. As a result, the next iteration of the GI Bill—the Veterans' Educational Assistance Program, or VEAP—was designed primarily to assist a peacetime military in recruitment. Passed in 1976, VEAP required servicemen and women to contribute between $25 and $100 a month to the program's education fund, to which the government would add double funds. Thus, if a service member contributed $100 a month to the VEAP fund, the government would kick in an additional $200 to reach the maximum benefit of $300. While initially consistent in real terms with the Vietnam GI Bill's benefits, the value of VEAP benefits deteriorated to roughly 60 percent of World War II benefits by the mid-1980s because of rampant inflation.[117]

In 1984, Congress passed the Montgomery GI Bill, named after bill sponsor Representative "Sonny" Montgomery of Mississippi, who had led the fight against compensation for Agent Orange victims. Like VEAP, which it wound up replacing, the Montgomery GI Bill is a contribution-based benefit. During the first 12 months of service, those service members wishing to take part in the GI Bill are required to contribute $100 a month. While the real value of Montgomery GI Bill benefits equaled those of VEAP when first implemented in the mid-1980s, by 2008 congressional action (most notably the 2001 Veterans Education and Benefits Expansion Act) raised benefits to levels comparable to those provided by the World War II GI Bill. Currently, Montgomery GI Bill benefits are indexed to increases in the Consumer Price Index.[118]

With wars in Iraq and Afghanistan placing unprecedented strain on America's armed forces and creating a new generation of veterans, Congress moved to create a new, expansive post-9/11 GI Bill of Rights. Spearheaded by Vietnam veteran Senators Chuck Hagel (R-NE) and Jim Webb (D-VA), the post-9/11 GI Bill provides all veterans who have served 90 days active duty after the 2001 terrorist attacks the full cost of tuition and fees at any public college or university, with as well as monetary living stipends and $1,000 a year for books. Significantly, unlike VEAP and the Montgomery GI Bill, the post-9/11 GI Bill does not require servicemen and women to make contributions. Any veteran who has served 36 months active duty is eligible for full benefits, including national guardsmen and reservists. According to the Iraq and Afghanistan Veterans of America, the average veteran would receive $18,815 in benefits in the program's first year.[119] Despite widespread bipartisan support for the Webb-Hagel measure, members of President George W. Bush's administration, including Secretary of Defense Robert Gates, argued that expanding benefits would hamper efforts to retain sufficient numbers of high-quality soldiers, sailors, airmen, and marines.[120] Despite administration opposition, Congress passed the post-9/11 GI Bill by landslide numbers—92 to 6 in the Senate and 416 to 12 in the House.[121] Facing overwhelming numbers, President Bush signed the post-9/11 GI Bill in to law on June 30, 2008.[122]

"I worry about this and what it says about our nation's view of the value of service," Senator Jim Webb remarked, commenting on the Bush administration's opposition to his post-9/11 GI Bill. "We hear from those opposed that it is too expensive and it's too complicated."[123] Indeed, as noted in this chapter, this argument has been heard from opponents of extending benefits to America's veterans since the beginning of the Republic. Whether it has been granting pensions to Revolutionary War veterans, expanding the GI Bill, or compensating for Agent Orange disabilities, veterans and their advocates have always had to contend with those focused more on controlling costs. Unfortunately, what America owes its veterans has always been a question decided by politics; it has never been a given proposition. Revolutionary War, World War I, and Vietnam veterans learned this the hard way, having to fight for their benefits. Civil War veterans skillfully manipulated partisan competition to securing larger and larger pensions, while World War II veterans relied on sympathetic figures within both executive and legislative branches of government and existing veterans organizations to secure the first GI Bill of Rights. Today's Iraq and Afghanistan veterans have learned well from history, forming their own pressure groups and leaning on friendly congresspersons. Unfortunately, the issue of proper compensation for America's veterans will never be a settled issue, but rather, as discussed in the next chapter, a constantly contested one. Future veterans and their allies should keep this history in mind.

Notes

1. Paul Dickson and Thomas B. Allen, *The Bonus Army: An American Epic* (New York: Walker and Company, 2004), 31

2. Wilbur Scott, *Vietnam Veterans Since the War: The Politics of PTSD, Agent Orange, and the National Memorial* (Norman: University of Oklahoma Press, 2004), 14.

3. Richard Severo and Lewis Milford, *The Wages of War: When America's Soldiers Came Home: From Valley Forge to Vietnam* (New York: Simon and Schuster, 1989), 32–33.

4. Richard Taylor, *Homeward Bound: American Veterans Return from War* (Westport, Conn.: Praeger, 2007), 13.

5. Severo and Milford, *The Wages of War,* 85.

6. Ibid., 85–90.

7. Department of Veterans Affairs, "History of the Department of Veterans Affairs—Part I," February 11, 2008, http://www1.va.gov/opa/feature/history/history1.asp.

8. Severo and Milford, *The Wages of War,* 91.

9. Department of Veterans Affairs, "History of the Department of Veterans Affairs—Part I."

10. Severo and Milford, *The Wages of War,* 92.

11. Department of Veterans Affairs, "History of the Department of Veterans Affairs—Part I."

12. Taylor, *Homeward Bound,* 23, 27–28.

13. Theda Skocpol, *Protecting Soldiers and Mothers: The Political Origins of Social Policy in the United States* (Cambridge, Mass.: Belknap Press, 1992), 103.

14. Department of Veterans Affairs, "History of the Department of Veterans Affairs—Part I."

15. Skocpol, *Protecting Soldiers,* 106–107.

16. Severo and Milford, *The Wages of War,* 136.

17. Department of Veterans Affairs, "History of the Department of Veterans Affairs—Part I."

18. Taylor, *Homeward Bound,* 54.

19. Severo and Milford, *The Wages of War,* 133–134.

20. Skocpol, *Protecting Soldiers,* 108–110.

21. Ibid., 115–116.

22. Ibid., 117.

23. Ibid., 120–121.

24. Ibid., 124–127.

25. Ibid., 128–129.

26. Department of Veterans Affairs, "History of the Department of Veterans Affairs—Part I."

27. Department of Veterans Affairs, "History of the Department of Veterans Affairs—Part 2," May 9, 2007, http://www1.va.gov/opa/feature/history/history2.asp; Department of Veterans Affairs, "History of US Government Involvement in Insurance," July 1, 2008, http://www.insurance.va.gov/inforceGLISite/generalinfo/InsHistory.htm; Dickson and Allen, *The Bonus Army,* 4, 20–21.

28. Dickson and Allen, *The Bonus Army,* 18–24.

29. Severo and Milford, *The Wages of War,* 247–249, 259.

30. Dickson and Allen, *The Bonus Army,* 27; Department of Veterans Affairs, "History of the Department of Veterans Affairs—Part 2."

31. Dickson and Allen, *The Bonus Army,* 25–27.

32. Ibid., 28–30.

33. Ibid., 34–38.

34. Ibid., 56–83.

35. Ibid., 94–95, 103–104, 118, 125–130.

36. Ibid., 137, 145–147, 149.

37. Ibid., 153–183.

38. Davis R. B. Ross, *Preparing for Ulysses: Politics and Veterans During World War II* (New York: Columbia University Press, 1969), 18–19.

39. Dickson and Allen, *The Bonus Army,* 230–231, 253–254, 262.

40. Ross, *Preparing for Ulysses,* 36–37.

41. Dickson and Allen, *The Bonus Army,* 19.

42. Ross, *Preparing for Ulysses,* 39–49.

43. Department of Veterans Affairs, "History of the Department of Veterans Affairs—Part 4," May 9, 2007, http://www1.va.gov/opa/feature/history/history4.asp.

44. U.S. Census Bureau, "Facts for Features: Special Edition Dedication of National World War II Memorial," April 29, 2004, http://www.census.gov/Press-Release/www/releases/archives/facts_for_features_special_editions/001747.html.

45. Ross, *Preparing for Ulysses,* 51–55.

46. Ibid., 56–58.

47. Suzanne Mettler, *Soldiers to Citizens: The G.I. Bill and the Making of the Greatest Generation* (New York: Oxford University Press, 2005), 17–19; Ross, *Preparing for Ulysses,* 61–63.

48. Franklin D. Roosevelt, "Fireside Chat on Progress of War and Plans for Peace," July 28, 1943, http://www.mhric.org/fdr/chat25.html.

49. Ibid.

50. Ross, *Preparing for Ulysses,* 68, 82–87.

51. Mettler, *Soldiers to Citizens,* 19–20; Ross, *Preparing for Ulysses,* 92–94.

52. Ross, *Preparing for Ulysses,* 98–99.

53. Ibid., 100–102.

54. Ibid., 96, 105–106.

55. Mettler, *Soldiers to Citizens,* 21–22; Ross, *Preparing for Ulysses,* 109.

56. Ross, *Preparing for Ulysses,* 117–118.

57. Department of Veterans Affairs, "History of the Department of Veterans Affairs—Part 4"; Mettler, *Soldiers to Citizens,* 6–7.

58. Mettler, *Soldiers to Citizens,* 61.

59. Ibid., 42–57, 104.

60. Ibid., 101–102.

61. Department of Veterans Affairs, "History of the Department of Veterans Affairs—Part 4."

62. Mettler, *Soldiers to Citizens,* 6.

63. Severo and Milford, *The Wages of War,* 304–306.

64. Department of Veterans Affairs, "History of the Department of Veterans Affairs—Part 5," May 9, 2007, http://www1.va.gov/opa/feature/history/history5.asp.

65. Severo and Milford, *The Wages of War,* 308–309.

66. Ross, *Preparing for Ulysses,* 279–280.

67. David P. Smole and Shannon S. Loane, "A Brief History of Veterans' Education Benefits and Their Value," *Congressional Research Service,* June 25, 2008, 3; Department of Veterans Affairs, "History of the Department of Veterans Affairs—Part 5."

68. Smole and Loane, "A Brief History," 3.

69. Department of Veterans Affairs, "History of the Department of Veterans Affairs—Part 6," May 9, 2007, http://www1.va.gov/opa/feature/history/history6.asp; Gerald Nicosia, *Home to War: A History of the Vietnam Veterans' Movement* (New York: Crown Publishers, 2001), 305.

70. Scott, *Vietnam Veterans,* 8.

71. Nicosia, *Home to War,* 199.

72. Scott, *Vietnam Veterans,* 11.

73. Nicosia, *Home to War,* 145–146, 317–319.

74. Nicosia, *Home to War,* 182–188; Scott, *Vietnam Veterans,* 4–5.

75. Nicosia, *Home to War,* 158–175.

76. Nicosia, *Home to War,* 193–194; Scott, *Vietnam Veterans,* 35–37.

77. Nicosia, *Home to War,* 202–209.

78. Scott, *Vietnam Veterans,* 38–39.

79. Nicosia, *Home to War,* 200.

80. Ibid., 305–307.

81. Ibid., 307–309, 325–334.

82. Ibid., 348–354.

83. Nicosia, *Home to War,* 362–368; Scott, *Vietnam Veterans,* 63–67.

84. Nicosia, *Home to War,* 506–510; Scott, *Vietnam Veterans,* 68–69.

85. Scott, *Vietnam Veterans,* 70–71

86. Department of Veterans Affairs, "Vet Center Home," May 27, 2008, http://www.vetcenter.va.gov/.

87. Nicosia, *Home to War,* 397–401.

88. Ibid., 423, 535–538.

89. Scott, *Vietnam Veterans,* 77–82.

90. Nicosia, *Home to War,* 487–488.

91. Scott, *Vietnam Veterans,* 81–82.

92. Nicosia, *Home to War,* 446.

93. Nicosia, *Home to War,* 386–387; Scott, *Vietnam Veterans,* 87–88.

94. Nicosia, *Home to War,* 388.

95. Scott, *Vietnam Veterans,* 89–90, 105–106.

96. Nicosia, *Home to War,* 388; Scott, *Vietnam Veterans,* 89–90.

97. Nicosia, *Home to War,* 487; Scott, *Vietnam Veterans,* 186–187.

98. Nicosia, *Home to War,* 452–454; Scott, *Vietnam Veterans,* 109–110.

99. Scott, *Vietnam Veterans,* 118.

100. Ibid., 165–166.

101. Nicosia, *Home to War,* 462.

102. Scott, *Vietnam Veterans,* 176–177.

103. Nicosia, *Home to War,* 590–591.

104. Scott, *Vietnam Veterans,* 199–200.

105. Nicosia, *Home to War,* 592–594.

106. Nicosia, *Home to War,* 597–601; Scott, *Vietnam Veterans,* 206–209.

107. Scott, *Vietnam Veterans,* 209–212.

108. Nicosia, *Home to War,* 602–604.

109. Scott, *Vietnam Veterans,* 222–223.

110. Nicosia, *Home to War,* 608–609, 612.

111. Ibid., 589–590, 616–617.

112. Research Advisory Committee on Gulf War Veterans' Illnesses, *Scientific Progress in Understanding Gulf War Veterans' Illnesses: Report and Recommendations,* September 2004, http://www1.va.gov/rac-gwvi/docs/ReportandRecommendations_2004.pdf, 5.

113. Department of Veterans Affairs, "Gulf War Review," May 2008, http://www1.va.gov/gulfwar/docs/GW_Review_May_2008.pdf, 5.

114. Andy Sullivan, "Gulf War Illness Is Real, Report Finds," *Reuters,* November 17, 2008, http://news.yahoo.com/s/nm/20081117/ts_nm/us_usa_health_gulfwar.

115. Smole and Loane, "A Brief History," 12–13.

116. Nicosia, *Home to War,* 305–306, 371–373.

117. Smole and Loane, "A Brief History," 3–4, 13.

118. Ibid., 4–5, 12–13.

119. "A New GI Bill: Rewarding Our Troops, Rebuilding Our Military," *GI Bill 2008,* http://gibill2008.org/sidebyside.html.

120. Charles M. Sennott, "GI Bill Falling Short of College Tuition Costs," *Boston Globe,* February 10, 2008, http://www.boston.com/news/nation/washington/articles/2008/02/10/gi_bill_falling_short_of_college_tuition_costs/.

121. Iraq and Afghanistan Veterans of America, "GI Bill Passes House 416–12," June 18, 2008, http://www.iava.org/component/option,com_/Itemid,67/option,content/task,view/id,2766/; Iraq and Afghanistan Veterans of America, "Landslide GI Bill Victory in the Senate (92–6)," June 27, 2008, http://www.iava.org/component/option,com_/Itemid,67/option,content/task,view/id,2771/.

122. George W. Bush, "President Bush Signs H.R. 2642, the Supplemental Appropriations Act, 2008," June 30, 2008, http://www.whitehouse.gov/news/releases/2008/06/20080630.html.

123. Sennott, "GI Bill Falling Short."

CHAPTER 3

The Impact of Veterans on the American Political System

Max A. Bergmann

While Social Security has often been described as the "third rail" of American politics—meaning that it is so politically popular that any effort to push reform would likely electrocute the reformer—the same can now probably be said of the VA system. But unlike Social Security few political leaders have argued for dramatically restructuring or overhauling the Department of Veterans Affairs (VA).

Over the last 30 years the Veterans Administration has survived relatively unscathed, and was perhaps even strengthened, in an era when the conservative vision of reducing the size of government dominated the political landscape. Ironically, the elevation of the Veterans Administration to cabinet-level status occurred in 1988 during the Reagan administration under pressure from Republican Senator Strom Thurmond of South Carolina. An administration that came into office pledging to eliminate government agencies closed its term by adding a new one. In the mid 1990s—despite the Republican revolution, which ushered in an era of conservative control of both the legislative and executive branches of government—a pledge to balance the budget and decrease the size of government by rolling back New Deal and Great Society entitlement programs, the new Department of Veterans Affairs was never seriously targeted for spending cuts. In fact, in 1981 when David Stockman, Reagan's first director of the Office of Management and Budget, proposed cutting $900 million from the VA budget, the Republican controlled Senate refused to support the reduction. This is even more surprising given that the VA is the second largest government agency, operates a massive government-run health care system, and provides extensive benefits to millions of Americans.

Instead, since the 1980s the two major political parties have engaged in an intense debate over who supports veterans and veterans benefits the most. Throughout each of the last four presidential campaigns, veterans benefits have become a prominent political topic. In each of these presidential elections each of the major party candidates has pledged to maintain or increase spending on veterans benefits.

The political clout of veterans groups helps explain much of the support for the VA system. Currently, there are about 24 million living veterans in the United States; but because their dependents are also eligible for benefits, an additional 37 million people must be included in this number. Together, this population amounts to about 20 percent of the U.S. populace. The growth of the VA did not happen without significant backing from powerful political groups. Highly organized and politically influential veterans groups, made up of a tremendously strong veterans lobby, work with Congress and its veterans committees, as well as the VA in the executive branch, to form an "iron triangle" that works to perpetuate and enhance veterans' benefits and veterans' interests.

This chapter will first provide a brief description of the Department of Veterans Affairs, demonstrating that this organization is a large piece of the American social safety net. The second section will explain the strength of the VA system and the "iron triangle" that supports it. The final section will examine the political debates during the VA's elevation to cabinet status in the late 1980s, the VA's situation during the 1994 Republican revolution, and the role of veterans' issues in each of the last four presidential elections. These examples demonstrate that the Veterans Administration is a strongly entrenched organization that, while often beset by management difficulties, holds a powerful political presence in American politics.

The VA System

As discussed in Chapter 2, Americans have a long history of providing various levels of support to veterans. Since the Civil War the U.S. has developed a large benefit and entitlement system designed specifically for individuals who served in the military. As Alec Campbell notes, "large scale twentieth century veterans' benefits are uniquely American. There is no French, British, German, Canadian, or Dutch, equivalent to the VA hospital system, the Veterans Housing Authority, or the GI Bill."[1] The VA boasts that "The United States has the most comprehensive system of assistance for veterans of any nation in the world."[2] With almost a fifth of the U.S. population now eligible to receive veterans benefits, the VA system developed a very large and often dysfunctional bureaucracy to administer such large benefit and entitlement programs. The Department of Veterans Affairs' annual budget of $90 billion and its more than 230,000 employees makes the Department of Veterans Affairs the largest government agency after the Department of Defense.

In 1988 the Veterans Administration, which had existed for about 50 years, was elevated to cabinet-level status and became the Department of Veterans Affairs. This has given the VA a seat at the table with the President and has meant that it is often included in broader policy discussions. It has also facilitated the growth of the VA's senior management, as the VA currently has 10 undersecretary and assistant secretary level positions in the department, while it only had three prior to gaining cabinet status. When one adds the position of secretary and deputy secretary, this means that the department has 12 positions that require Senate confirmation.

The Department of Veterans Affairs is presently composed of three separate entities: the Veterans Health Administration (VHA), the Veterans Benefit Administration (VBA), and the National Cemetery Administration (NCA). The VHA is the largest of the three and accounts for nearly half of the VA's budget. The VHA operates a nationwide network of 153 hospitals, 895 outpatient clinics, 135 nursing homes, 47 residential rehabilitation treatment programs, and 209 readjustment counseling centers. In 2007, the VHA provided health care to more than five million veterans. The VHA describes itself as "among the largest providers of health professional training in the world; operates one of the largest and most effective research organizations in the United States; is a principal federal asset for providing medical assistance in major disasters; and serves as the largest direct-care provider for homeless citizens in the United States."[3] Presently, the VHA provides care at more than 1,400 sites throughout the country, employs a staff of over 200,000, and maintains affiliations with 107 academic health systems. A full two-thirds of all physicians practicing in the U.S. today have trained in VA facilities.

The second part of the VA system, the VBA, receives more than half of the VA's budget and sends out more than $44 billion in checks out to veterans and their dependents each year. The VBA distributes benefits to veterans who were disabled while serving, to the survivors of service members who died on active duty or while serving in combat, and pension benefits to low income veterans. It also has several other functions. The VBA administers the GI bill and other education benefits. The VBA also offers home loans and helps provide assistance to veterans struggling to meet their payments. It provides insurance, including life insurance, mortgage insurance and disability insurance. Finally, it provides employment counseling and administers programs that help to integrate veterans back into the work force. To do this, the Veterans Benefits Administration (VBA) operates 57 regional offices.

The third part of the VA, the NCA accounts for a fairly small portion of the budget and operates 125 national cemeteries.[4] The NCA provides internment services to veterans and provides the headstones, markers, and inscription for veterans' cemeteries in the United States and around the world.

To maintain such a large health care and benefit system, the VA has a substantial budget. Since World War I, the VA's budget, measured in constant dollars, has historically increased dramatically immediately following conflicts and then has gradually tapered off. The VA's budget has risen in this decade to meet the growing demand for its services from the millions of veterans returning from the Iraq and Afghanistan wars. Between 2007 and 2008, for instance, the budget of the VA increased by almost 10 percent from $82 billion in 2007 to $90 billion in 2008. However, many veterans groups have argued that with the growth in the cost of medical care overall, the VA's budget has not risen fast enough to meet the increased demand. Yet, even when measured in constant dollars, the VA's budget is now as large as it was in the aftermath of World War II.[5]

The persistence of this large and growing entitlement and benefit system challenges the notion that the American system is inherently averse to such large "social welfare state" programs as a nationalized health care system. Alec Campbell notes, "When one accounts for Civil War pensions, the American welfare state no longer appears as a miserly late developer but rather as a precocious spendthrift. The same is true in the twentieth century." Campbell adds that many of the large entitlement programs that are now pillars of the American safety net were preceded by programs for veterans. "Federally funded health care did not begin with Medicaid and Medicare. Affirmative Action aided veterans in the civil service long before it aided racial minorities and women in the labor market; the educational provisions of the GI bill were the first major assistance to college students. Twentieth-century veterans' benefits prefigured Great Society programs just as Civil War pensions prefigured Social Security."[6] Campbell concludes that "veterans' benefits force a reconsideration of the standard narrative of American welfare state development which emphasizes the two "big bangs" or the New Deal and the Great Society."[7]

This begs the question of how such large welfare state benefit and entitlement programs have developed in the United States, seemingly under the radar and without significant debate, when other social welfare programs—such as universal health care, welfare benefits, and social security—have been and still are at the center of heated political debates in the United States. One explanation is that America is a country that highly values individualism and self-reliance. Therefore there is a strong sense of obligation and gratitude felt by the public and political leaders toward those individuals that have voluntarily or been forced to put themselves in harm's way on behalf of their country. This helps to explain why after wars the U.S. government has often dramatically increased its level of support to veterans, for example by expanding educational benefits through GI bills. But it does not fully explain the large and entrenched nature of the VA system.

The Iron Triangle: Veterans, Congress, and the VA

The VA has proved incredibly durable. Even during times when the objective of the party in power was to shrink the size of government, and large government agencies were stigmatized as socialist style bureaucracies, the VA was largely spared such scorn. The development of the VA was aided by the tremendous support it receives from voluntary public organizations, like the American Legion and Veterans of Foreign Wars, that have great influence on Capitol Hill and support from the executive branch. Like the military industrial complex, this creates an "iron triangle" relationship where the interaction among the bureaucracy or government agencies, congress, and interest groups is exceptionally strong. Central to this concept is the idea that government agencies seek to develop a strong relationship with politically active members or groups that share the same general interests or goals. Agencies seek to establish these constituent relationships in order to expand their political clout and to increase their share of the budgetary pie. The interest groups use their influence to lobby congress, providing political or electoral support in return for support on a given issue. This alliance is very stable and is a clear depiction of the power structure supporting the VA.

Voluntary associations and interest groups have long had a central place in American politics. French liberal aristocrat Alexis de Tocqueville marveled at the vibrancy of American civil society, noting the exceptional number of voluntary associations when he toured America in the 1830s. These voluntary associations often have influence that is unrivaled anywhere else in the world. America's political system was designed without political parties in mind. This has resulted in a system of "weak" parties, where members of Congress have significant autonomy from their party leadership, especially compared to parliamentary democracies. In parliamentary systems, the leadership of the political party usually has tremendous control over who stands for election and maintains rigid control over the agenda. The relative autonomy allotted to legislators in the American political system provides space for voluntary civic organizations to play an influential role. Legislators often need the support and funding from outside groups to bolster their reelection efforts, which makes them prone to support the causes of well organized and financed groups. Additionally, because of our weak party system legislators often seek guidance outside the party leadership on issues with which they have little familiarity. They may also seek to consult and work with an outside organization to draft legislation on that organization's area of expertise. Civil society organizations, like the National Rifle Association, the Sierra Club, and pro-choice groups like NARAL, at times play a very influential role in passing or blocking congressional legislation. In return for this influence, these interest groups provide political or financial support to the members.

The influence of outside groups has frequently become a political issue in and of itself. In the early 1900s the influence of powerful business monopolies known as trusts and their efforts to block many political reforms became an important issue and a rallying cry of President Theodore Roosevelt, who pledged to take them on, saying trust-busting would be one of his major priorities. In the 2008 election, then Senator Obama pledged to combat the power of special-interest lobbyists in Washington and put restrictions on including lobbyists in his campaign. Such organizations and individuals are criticized for being overly focused on their own narrow interests without considering the larger interests of the country and sometimes even at the expense of the common good.

However, many point out that these groups usually counter each other, as gun control advocates will run up against gun rights advocates, resulting in a vibrant political debate that serves to organize and inform the public. However, as former Illinois Congressman Edward J. Derwinski, the Secretary of the Department of Veterans Affairs during the administration of President George H. W. Bush, explained, veterans groups have "one unique edge... There is no anti-veterans group... It's just a one way street."[8] The absence of any organized opposition, combined with the extensive national presence of veterans groups like the Veterans of Foreign Wars (VFW) and the American Legion, which are embedded in communities throughout the country, has made veterans groups an extremely potent political force. Veterans groups, with their alliance with the VA and close connection to veterans committees in Congress, form a text-book "iron triangle" of interest groups, with the bureaucracy and the Congress.

In 1988 the Veterans Administration was elevated to a cabinet-level agency, giving it a full seat at the table with the President. The increased status was reflective of the influence of the veterans lobby throughout all levels of government, since the elevation was supported by the executive branch as well as the legislative arm. The Veterans Administration already had tremendous influence, but the enhanced prestige derived from cabinet stature meant the Department of Veterans Affairs' effectiveness in advocating for the growth in its funding would increase. Just as the Department of Defense has an intensive legislative outreach operation that seeks to persuade Congress to move in certain directions, so does the VA. Like the Pentagon, the Department of Veterans Affairs has an assistant secretary position devoted to congressional and legislative affairs. Additionally, the Secretary of Veterans Affairs is almost always a veteran who often has substantial experience working with veterans groups. This means that there is often a close alignment between the VA and the veterans interest groups. An opinion article in the *St. Petersburg Times* in 1987, on the issue of elevating the VA's status to cabinet-level, analyzed the clout of these organizations. "On Capitol Hill, both houses of Congress have committees on veterans affairs. At the beginning of each session of Congress these committees set aside hearing days for each of the major veterans organizations—the American Legion, the VFW, the Disabled American Veterans, and so on. Leaders of these groups tell committee members—their congressmen—what they would like Congress and the government to do for veterans during the year ahead. No other segment of the population receives such hospitable treatment from the United States government. Certainly not taxpayers."[9]

There are many different types of veterans groups. Some are focused on providing logistical support and consoling services to veterans and play only a limited legislative role; others work exclusively to advocate and advance veterans' concerns and issues. Two of the oldest and most influential veterans organizations are the American Legion and the VFW. The American Legion is the largest veterans group. It was chartered by Congress in 1919 to act as a "as a patriotic, war-time veterans organization, devoted to mutual helpfulness." It is a non-profit organization that is open to anyone who has served in the military and has almost three million members with about 15,000 posts worldwide.[10] Its headquarters are in Indianapolis, Indiana, but it has additional offices in Washington, DC and a staff of around 300 full-time employees.

Similarly, the VFW has 2.2 million members and approximately 8,100 posts. The VFW, which as its name implies, recruits only those who have served in a combat zone, came into being after the Spanish-American War in 1898, as many veterans arrived home in need of medical care and assistance but received little help. The VFW is focused on lobbying on behalf of veterans. Their mission statement says that its purpose is to "honor the dead by helping the living." The VFW puts tremendous energy into work-ing to assist veterans and lobby on behalf of their issues and concerns.[11]

The VFW has significant influence on Capitol Hill, as the VFW itself boasts. "The VFW's presence on Capitol Hill allows VFW officials to moni-tor and lobby Congress for legislative action targeted toward maintaining a strong national defense and improving military benefits and quality of life for all veterans, including those currently serving in the active duty military, the National Guard and the Reserves. The VFW has played an instrumental role in nearly every piece of veterans legislation passed in the 20th century, as well as bills developed in the 21st."[12] One of the VFW's most successful legislative pushes was making college education afford-able for military service members with the enactment of the 1944 GI Bill of Rights, the Montgomery GI Bill in 1984, and the new 21st century GI Bill in 2008.[13]

Both organizations, while nonpartisan, tend to have a conservative ap-proach to the political issues of the day. For instance, the American Legion is a very strong advocate for a constitutional amendment to ban flag burn-ing. In 2007, the American Legion and the VFW injected themselves into the ferocious political debate over the surge in Iraq. As the *Boston Globe* noted in the summer of 2007, "The American Legion and the Veterans of Foreign Wars, the nation's oldest and most influential veterans' organiza-tions, have broken their relative silence on the merits of the Iraq war, joining some of the staunchest war supporters to lobby Congress and the public to give the military 'surge' more time to work... Both organizations, which the [George W. Bush] White House has aggressively courted, have recently issued pro-war position statements and lobbied skeptical Repub-licans to back the current Iraq strategy. They are also recruiting members to argue for the surge strategy at town hall meetings, and have made their leaders available to the national media to declare that victory is still within reach."[14]

New veterans organizations have also recently emerged in the midst of the wars in Iraq and Afghanistan. The rise of the Internet and the in-creased connectivity it creates has had a tremendous impact on the ability of people to organize and connect with one another. This has certainly been the case for veterans. New veterans groups, made up of younger vets recently returned from Iraq or Afghanistan, have developed organizations that instead of relying on the system of offices and posts to organize and engage their members as the American Legion and VFW do, have utilized the Internet. Unlike the American Legion and the VFW, these new veter-ans groups have developed on both sides of the political spectrum, many emerged to oppose the war in Iraq. Since many of the large and existing veterans organizations took a favorable view toward the war in Iraq, there was a considerable vacuum for veterans groups that opposed the war to come into being. With many returning veterans upset by what they had seen as a poorly managed and a strategically inept approach in Iraq, new organizations emerged to capture this discontent in an effort to organize opposition to the war.

One of the most prominent groups to emerge after 9/11 is the Iraq and Afghanistan Veterans of America (IAVA). The IAVA was formed in 2004 and it is the first and largest veterans organization for the veterans of the wars in Iraq and Afghanistan. The IAVA takes a neutral stance toward the war, but it is a forceful advocate on behalf of veterans, as well as on issues relating to the wars in Iraq and Afghanistan. Although the organization has adopted a more neutral stance toward the war in Iraq, its founder and executive director Paul Rieckhoff, an army veteran of the Iraq war, has been an outspoken critic of the war in Iraq and the Bush administration. The IAVA has highlighted the deleterious impact of the wars in Iraq and Afghanistan on the ground forces and has pointed to the need to address equipment shortages, such as the lack of adequate body and vehicle armor. In 2007, following the American Legion and the VFW's endorsement of the war in Iraq, Rieckhoff said "They are choosing to point their organizations in a certain direction, but they have failed to capture the new generation of veterans." Reickhoff added that, in his view, the American Legion and VFW's outspokenness on the surge "compromises their ability to advocate on behalf of veterans."[15]

The IAVA has a detailed legislative agenda and is heavily engaged in lobbying congress. It has pushed aggressively for the new 21st-century GI Bill. In laying out its priorities for 2008 the IAVA explained that the coming fight over the GI bill would be central to their efforts in 2008:

> The cornerstone of IAVA's 2008 Legislative Agenda is a new GI Bill for today's service members. Extensive research, congressional testimony and meetings with key lawmakers have set the groundwork for a comprehensive campaign that will utilize all of IAVA's assets to advocate for a World War II-style GI Bill. A companion website, www. GIBill2008.org, serves as the campaign center, where users can send a letter to their Senator or Representative urging him or her to support a new GI bill, learn more about its history and why action is needed. IAVA will mobilize veterans in key districts and states across the country to put pressure on Congress and the President, and submit letters to the editor and op-eds to their local newspapers. The GI Bill is a vital investment in a new generation of leaders, and its

passage would demonstrate that this nation respects and honors their service. Visit www.GIBill2008.org for the latest updates in this historic movement.[16]

Additionally, the IAVA developed a scorecard to rate legislators on their support for veterans' issues. It proclaimed that, "the scorecard will be a comprehensive guide to legislators' performance on issues that affect the lives of America's troops, veterans, and military families. The IAVA's nationwide network of Iraq and Afghanistan veterans has expressed overwhelmingly consistent positions on issues ranging from VA funding and veterans' education benefits to body armor and TRICARE health insurance for Guard and Reserve troops. The IAVA will use these positions to determine whether each member of Congress has been a friend, or foe, of our men and women in uniform."[17] Devices like a voting scorecard put tremendous pressure on legislators, as they are all conscious that these can easily be used by their political opponents in coming elections.

Similarly, another organization, Veterans for America (VFA), also seeks to provide support for veterans of the current wars. The VFA, also known as the Vietnam Veterans of America Foundation (VVAF), and it attempts to "unite the current generation of service members and veterans with veterans from previous wars [in order] to address the needs of our men and women in uniform—both active-duty and Guard/Reserve—and their families. The VFA's mission is to ensure that the voices of those who have sacrificed immeasurably on behalf our country in recent years are heard and that support commensurate with their sacrifice is provided."[18] The VFA places much emphasis in their legislative focus on the need to increase efforts to deal with those veterans suffering from traumatic brain injuries and psychological trauma. "VFA focuses specifically on the signature wounds these conflicts: psychological traumas and traumatic brain injuries. VFA concentrates much of its attention on the needs of those who are currently serving in the military since the majority of those who have seen combat in Iraq and Afghanistan are still in the military and under the care of the Department of Defense."[19]

During the 2006 election a group called VoteVets, an organization made up of veterans who had recently returned from Iraq and Afghanistan, led by charismatic Iraq war veteran Jon Soltz and backed by retired General and former presidential candidate Wesley Clark, burst on the political scene with highly politically charged advertisements that attacked Republican politicians engaged in tough reelection fights, for not allocating funds to provide enough body armor to the troops serving in Iraq. VoteVets is also very active in advancing veterans' issues. VoteVets advocates fully funding "the Department of Veterans Affairs, so that every Veteran seeking care has fast and convenient access to it." VoteVets notes that, "the VA has been consistently under-funded by billions of dollars. This has resulted in the closing of VA clinics, limited medical equipment, and long delays before receiving medical care."[20]

VoteVets has both a non-partisan 501c(4) "action fund" side, as well as its own political action committee. The 501c(4) designation refers to an organization's tax status. This status enables VoteVets to use tax deductible contributions to organize advocacy campaigns, whereby it can encourage its members to call their congressman, sign letters, and engage in other organizational activities that lobby or advocate on behalf of a certain view point. 501c(4) organizations are officially designated as non-partisan organizations, as they do not advocate a specific party but a view point. VoteVets is funded through outside donors—similar to most of Washington D.C.'s think tanks. Like Washington think tanks, funding for VoteVets and similar veterans groups comes largely from one side of the political spectrum. While VoteVets is a nonpartisan organization, it aggressively advocates ending the war in Iraq and providing increased benefits for veterans, which puts it ideologically in close alignment with the Democratic Party. VoteVets also developed a political action committee that supports veterans running for office that subscribe to their views, which has meant that it has largely supported Democratic candidates. However, it has also supported Republican candidates who have opposed the war in Iraq. But its political efforts, most notably its advertisements, have been used against pro-war Republican candidates, such as Georgia Senator Saxby Chambliss in 2008 and former Senator George Allen of Virginia, who in 2006 lost to decorated Vietnam veteran and former Navy Secretary Jim Webb—a candidate aggressively supported by VoteVets. During the 2008 presidential election VoteVets was very active in opposing Senator McCain. It strongly critiqued his record on veterans' issues and his stance on the Iraq war, as well as his hawkish position on Iran.

In response to the development of strongly progressive veterans groups, the conservative right helped create a new younger veterans organization called Vets for Freedom to counter organizations like VoteVets. Vets for Freedom chairman Pete Hegseth, like VoteVets Chairman Jon Soltz, has been highly active in the current political debates and has been made frequent appearances on radio and TV and written several op-eds.

However, Vets for Freedom was more narrowly focused on promoting President Bush's surge strategy for Iraq rather than lobbying on behalf of veterans' issues. Vets for Freedom's mission statement says the organization's purpose is to "educate the American public about the importance of achieving success in these conflicts by applying our first-hand knowledge to issues of American strategy and tactics in Iraq."[21]

Vets for Freedom was officially established in November 2007, following the 2006 congressional elections in which Iraq was an issue of critical importance. Their mission statement reflects the organization's focus on supporting the war in Iraq. Vets for Freedom does not take an active role in promoting veterans legislation. For example, prior to the final vote on the 21st-century GI Bill, Vets for Freedom released a press release that urged a more nuanced approach toward the bill. The press release read, "Vets For Freedom urges Senate members to work together to pass a GI Bill that not only addresses the immediate need for increased financial and educational benefits, but that also takes into account the unique dynamics of today's all-volunteer force."[22] This stance was supportive of Senator McCain's position on the bill, which opposed the bill on the grounds that the new GI bill would create retention difficulties for the armed forces, because in his view, the bill's extensive benefits creates incentives to leave the services. Vets for Freedom's position made them an outlier compared to most veterans groups.

The influence of the many veterans groups has been greatly aided by the fact that support for veterans benefits has tended to be very popular with the general public—something that has not been lost on electorally minded members of congress. Proposing cuts in veterans benefits or in the Department of Veterans Affairs is therefore exceptionally difficult politically. Conversely, supporting increases in funding is often incredibly politically popular or at the very least has the prospect of gaining the support of a large and influential constituency. Therefore veterans' issues have strong support on Capitol Hill, where congressional leaders often attempt to outdo each other in demonstrating their support for veterans.

For instance, in the early 1990s the George H. W. Bush administration sought to end surgery at 33 small VA hospitals. The VA Inspector General found in a 1991 report that, at small VA hospitals, doctors rarely performed surgery and when they did they were prone to mistakes. However, Congress responded harshly to the administration's proposal. Tom Daschle, then a Democratic congressman from South Dakota and future Senate Majority leader, along with Senator Max Baucus, a Democrat from Montana, mocked the notion that hospitals in their states were unsafe. Thus, out of the 33 hospital surgical units only three were closed. The head of the VA medical system, James W. Holsinger, Jr., explained that the effort may have been a "bigger bag of worms than anybody wanted to deal with . . . The problem is that people engaged in the process are not necessarily patients. They are the leadership of [veterans groups], political leaders in an area. There are questions of identity, issues of civic pride."[23]

After World War II, 10 percent of the population were made up of veterans, and the size of the veterans population grew continuously until the United States ended the draft in 1973. As Alec Campbell notes, "In the twentieth century and particularly after 1945, military service was one of the most common shared experiences of American men. As a result, benefits reached a large part of the population and certainly were as widespread as Civil War pensions."[24] As the veterans population declines with the deaths of World War II veterans and the shift to a smaller all-volunteer military, one might expect a decline in the power of the veterans lobby. Additionally, the decreasing number of elected political leaders who have served in the military might also lead to a decreasing concern for veterans' issues. But thus far this has not been the case. If anything, the volunteer nature of military service creates extra pressure to give back to those who serve and to fulfill the commitments made to those who volunteered. Pressures are often placed on politicians who have not served to prove their support for the military and therefore to veterans. The most common route to demonstrate such support is by favoring increasing VA benefits and demonstrating a strong record of support for vets.

Veterans' Issues in the American Political Debate

Veterans' issues have had an important place in American political debates over the last two decades. The two major parties have tended to both be very supportive. However, there are ideological differences. Some conservative Republicans see the VA system as an example of a bloated big government bureaucracy and thus have frequently advocated reform or at the very least resisted funding increases. Democrats, on the other hand, have generally tended to be more supportive of the concept of government programs and have frequently advocated expanding veterans programs. The debates over the VA's cabinet status, the place of the VA following the 1994 Republican revolution, and its role throughout the last four presidential elections, have all demonstrated the tremendous strength of veterans groups and the political popularity of these issues amongst the general public.

Debate over the VA's Cabinet Status

The debate in the late 1980s over elevating the Veterans Administration to full cabinet-level status pitted those ideologically committed to the cause of smaller government against the powerful influence of veterans groups. The argument against making the VA a cabinet-level agency was not based on the question whether or how to care for veterans, but over the nature of government. Opponents argued that elevating its status was just another case of the government growing out of control. *New York Times* conservative columnist William Safire, a speechwriter for President Nixon, called veterans benefits a "sacred cow" while others worried that making the VA a cabinet-level agency would only enhance the already incredibly powerful veterans lobby and would lead to a rapidly growing entitlement program. Proponents on the other hand have argued that such a large governmental organization that impacted so many should have a seat at the table with the president.

President Reagan announced his decision to elevate the Veterans Administration, saying "There is no better time or better way to salute those valiant men and women than to announce today my decision to support the creation of a Cabinet-level Department of Veterans Affairs... This is a personal decision that I have thought about for some time," he said. "Veterans have always had a strong voice in our government. It's time to give them the recognition they so rightly deserve."[25] The decision surprised members of congress who were lobbying on behalf of cabinet status for the VA. Representative Gerald B. Solomon, Republican of upstate New York and ranking Republican on the veterans' committee told President Reagan, "This is the first time you've ever tricked me. We came here to have to sell you a bill of goods and you were already sold. Thank you."[26] The measure had tremendous bipartisan support. Representative G. V. (Sonny) Montgomery, Democrat of Mississippi, the chairman of the House Veterans Affairs Committee, known on Capitol Hill as "Mr. Veteran," was also very supportive of the elevation. The effort to elevate the VA to cabinet-level was not confined to the Reagan administration or the 1986 congress. A bill to change the VA's status had been introduced in the previous 17 Congresses going back to 1952.[27]

The push to elevate the Veterans Administration to a cabinet-level agency and to make the head of the VA a cabinet secretary originated from veterans groups outside of government, such as the Vietnam Veterans of America.[28] The argument for elevating the status of the VA was that it would give it more clout and would give the head of the VA more access to the president at a time when the budget for veterans was in danger of being squeezed by soaring deficits. There was growing anger that veterans were being forced to pay for portions of their treatment to the VA hospitals. The *Economist* magazine assessed that part of the push for the change occurred because of increasing encroachments into VA activities.

As the largest independent agency in the government with constitu-
ents in every city and county, the VA makes its presence felt. Until
recently, its budget was growing inexorably, as the large group of ex-
servicemen from the Second World War grew older and less hale.
Until recently, it awarded benefits with unbridled generosity, never
asking whether the recipients could afford to pay for treatment or
not. The rules have now become stricter. In April, Congress required
some ex-servicemen to pay for part of their treatment, and the latest
Reagan budget suggested that those with an income of more than
$15,000 should not get free health benefits at all. It is probably these
small encroachments on the agency's charitable empire, rather than
the empire's sheer size that have driven some ex-servicemen to feel
they must make more noise, if possible in the cabinet.[29]

Many advocates for the change argued that the VA was being marginal-
ized by a strong Office of Management and Budget (OMB) and its director, David Stockman. The VA's budget allocation was overseen by OMB.
"Mr. Veteran," Sonny Montgomery, commented at the time of Reagan's announcement that "Some feel the V.A. is run now by the Office of Management and Budget."[30] His Republican colleague on the committee, Gerald
Solomon, noted that, "Right now we have to go through the back door at
the White House . . . We are going to eliminate that with this Cabinet-level
position."[31] Solomon was upset that the VA was "at the mercy of the president's Office of Management and Budget, with the result that the agency's
hospital system is suffering from "a $600 million shortfall."[32]

Yet increasing the clout of the VA and removing it from under the OMB
was exactly what opponents of the change were afraid of. In 1988 the VA
had 220,000 employees, making it the largest agency after the Department
of Defense and it had more facilities around the country than any agency
with the exception of the Postal Service. At the time, it impacted 27 million
veterans and 51 million dependants, approximately one-third of the total
population.[33] In 1982 the VA operated 172 hospitals, 117 nursing homes
and 230 outpatient clinics, and it maintained 111 national cemeteries.
It had an annual budget of more than $27 billion, and spent more than
$15 billion a year on benefits programs to veterans and their dependents.[34]

Reagan's announcement was widely criticized by many of his supporters, who noted that Reagan was elected in 1980 on his hostility to increasing the size of the government. Reagan had previously opposed the
creation of new federal agencies, such as the Department of Education
under President Carter. In his successful campaign for the White House
in 1980, Reagan even pledged to eliminate the two newest cabinet-level
agencies, the departments of Education and Energy. Instead, the Reagan

administration eliminated neither, and with the elevation of the VA was actually seeking to add another. A *New York Times* editorial explained that the problem of:

> consistency confronts President Reagan. He embraces the idea of departmentalizing the Veterans Administration...Yet in 1980, he promised to "get the Government off our backs" and to abolish the two latest departments, Energy and Education. Now, instead of rolling back the number from 13 to 11, he welcomes No. 14. With a stroke of the pen, President Reagan could eliminate all three problems: of consistency, precedent and memory. Instead of signing the Veterans Department bill, he could use another V-word. Veto.[35]

John R. Block, Reagan's Secretary of Agriculture from 1981 to 1986, summed up the feelings of many Reaganites when he said with anguish, "Although I am a West Point graduate and believe in a strong military and support veterans organizations, I can see absolutely no justification for another Cabinet department... There are too many secretaries sitting around that Cabinet table now. Too many advocates in the Cabinet room advising the President confuse the issues and are counterproductive. The consequences of a bulging Cabinet will ultimately force the President to rely more and more on White House staff in private meetings and less on his Cabinet in Cabinet meetings. I cannot think of a worse idea."[36]

Republican Congressman John Edward Porter of Illinois protested that "This is being considered when we are bleeding red ink.... Veterans are a very powerful special interest in this country and members are in craven fear of retribution at the polls."[37] In response to this line of attack, Reagan officials downplayed the importance of the measure. A spokesman for President Reagan said changing the designation of the VA "would not necessarily increase its size or budget but would give it a greater say in the councils of government and would make it an active and working part of the President's Cabinet."[38] The Reagan administration argued that the elevation would have little impact on the budget and John Sholzen put the additional cost merely at $30,000 mainly to provide salary increases for the Administrator and other top officials.[39] The Congressional Budget Office projected the cost of the move would be negligible.[40]

A study by the National Academy of Public Administration agreed that the impact would be minimal, but concluded saying it found "little evidence that the vital mission of providing for the present and future needs of our veterans would be materially improved" by the proposal.[41] The General Accounting Office or GAO (now called the Government

Accountability Office) similarly argued that the VA's management problems were more of a problem than its status.[42]

But conservatives were worried that bestowing cabinet-level status on the VA was providing legitimacy to broader state-welfare programs. Columnist William Safire called the VA a "Trojan horse" and wrote in the *New York Times,*

> Never glorify Big Government. Never let it win the battle of symbols, because then it will win the war of the budget. When the decision memo went to the President on the big-spenders' plan to elevate the V.A. to cabinet status, the White House staff made the customary conservative recommendation: It's a Trojan horse to infiltrate the Government with new entitlements for the baby boomers, so shoot it down. But Ronald Reagan, influenced by patronage-hungry Senator Strom Thurmond, signed on to the scheme... Does anyone imagine that the vast new clout given the professional veterans' lobby will not cost all taxpayers (including vets not seeking the public trough) billions in the future? This is Washington; a place at the cabinet table cannot fail to put bread on the constituency's table.[43]

However, Max Cleland, a triple amputee from the war in Vietnam, was supportive of the effort to elevate the VA's status. Cleland served as the head of the VA in the Carter administration and was given access to the White House when Carter signed an executive order allowing Cleland to sit in on Cabinet meetings—an act that the Reagan administration did not continue. Cleland said "I sat in the cheap seats around the wall. I didn't sit at the table with the president," adding that he was not a full member of the Cabinet. But he said Carter's decision opened "my window to the world, not only providing insight into what the president was thinking and what was happening in the federal government but, more importantly, insight into what I and my agency could do to serve America's defenders and their families. In contrast, when a VA administrator does not have access to the president and to the functions of the government, he can find himself—and the agency—isolated in the bureaucracy and getting 'lost in the shuffle,' ultimately causing the agency and its mission to suffer."[44] This argument was powerful and the general feeling was captured by Representative Jack Brooks, a Democrat from Texas who managed the House bill, who said, "This is a great deal, and it's not going to do any harm to anybody."

While there was bipartisan support for the measure in congress, a congressional staffer noted that "There's practically unanimous editorial opinion that this shouldn't be done.[45] The proposal was widely condemned by editorial boards around the country. The editorials argued that the VA was largely an administrative organization that did not need a seat at the policy making table. The *New York Times* wrote as the proposal made its way through congress:

> Elevating the Veterans Administration to cabinet status is an idea that doesn't improve with age...But the legislators don't need any persuasion, it seems. They are stampeding to enact the bill...Ronald Reagan, that implacable foe of big government, touched off the stampede. Bills to create a cabinet-level V.A. have been dutifully introduced in every Congress for the last quarter-century and then wisely allowed to languish and die.... Cabinet status is not a way of conferring "recognition" on deserving groups; that's what monuments and memorials are for. Cabinet status is to designate broad areas of policy that regularly require the chief executive's attention. The work of the Veterans Administration, 99 percent of it simply administrative, does not fit that description. And to the extent that veterans' matters do require policy attention, it is as a facet of Pentagon policy. Veterans' benefits are basically a form of deferred compensation for military service...Veterans programs now touch almost 80 million Americans, including 27 million actual veterans. They make up a vocal and potent constituency, and that explains better than anything else why the scheme for a cabinet-level V.A. is advancing on Capitol Hill.[46]

The *Washington Post* agreed. Its editors noted, "Writing checks and running hospitals and cemeteries for the nation's veterans are purely administrative duties, in no way comparable. If the V.A.'s status is to be changed, it logically would be absorbed into the Department of Defense. Veterans' benefits are, after all, merely a form of deferred compensation for military personnel."[47]

The *Christian Science Monitor* argued that the VA was already powerful and already had an advocate at cabinet-level. "Reagan's proposal to elevate the Veterans Administration into a Cabinet-level department may have a lot of political appeal. Little wonder: There are about 28 million veterans in the United States. And they vote. Still, the plan is unnecessary and should be given thumbs down...The underlying issue is really about power...The Veterans Administration already has clout to spare. And an ally in the Cabinet. That ally is the Pentagon, which, when last we noted, also spoke out on issues affecting people in—or once in—uniforms."[48] The *St. Petersburg Times* ran an irate op-ed by a World War II veteran titled, "Reagan's Plan for Veterans is FUBAR":

> On one particular question, President Reagan is FUBAR. Any veteran of World War II will understand the acronym: FUBAR—fouled up

beyond all recognition. It's apt because the question relates to veterans. On the day before Veterans Day, as he met in the Cabinet room of the White House with leaders of the major veterans' organizations and their congressmen, the president said he favors the creation of a Cabinet-level Department of Veterans Affairs... If the VA and veterans require any "greater say in the councils of government," the need is not apparent... That is why it was confusing to hear the president say, "It's time to give them the recognition they so rightly deserve." He's FUBAR. His priorities are scrambled.[49]

The number of political appointees was one stumbling block in congressional approval for the cabinet status, as many in congress feared that this would politicize the agency. The head of the VA at the time of its elevation, Thomas K. Turnage, told the Senate Governmental Affairs Committee that the new department should have up to 12 presidential appointees, when—at the time—they only had three at the agency. Turnage justified this increase saying it would give the VA "greater flexibility." Harry Walters, who preceded Turnage as Reagan's VA administrator, told the Committee that the increase in presidential nominees would be good for the VA since "the confirmation process would give the Senate a chance to look at the credentials of the appointees."[50] But Sen. John Heinz (R-PA) scoffed, saying that this is just "one more instance of the VA wanting a free hand to do anything it wants." And Max Cleland said that he thought the Senate confirmation for three appointees, the administrator, deputy administrator and inspector general, was "quite adequate."[51] Today, the Department of Veterans Affairs has 12 presidential appointments for positions of the assistant secretaries, undersecretary, deputy secretary, and secretary.

But the power of the veterans lobby was simply too strong. The measure passed the House almost unanimously by a vote of 399 to 17 and Reagan signed it into law on October 25, 1988 to take effect in March of 1989, two months after he was to leave office. The *New York Times* glumly pointed out that Congress had set a bad precedent. "Having discovered how much some special interests love the recognition of a seat at the Cabinet table, some members are eager to departmentalize others, like the Environmental Protection Agency and the National Aeronautics and Space Administration. If there's space in the Cabinet for Space, where will Congress draw the line?"[52]

It is difficult to determine the exact impact of making the VA a cabinet-level position. The VA's budgets increased only very gradually throughout the 1990s. About 13 years after the Department of Veterans Affairs came into being, Donald Kettle, then professor of political science at the University of Wisconsin, said that President Ronald Reagan's elevation of the

Veterans Administration to the cabinet-level "didn't require much more than repainting the signs and reprinting the letterhead."[53] But it did to some extent legitimize the VA system and its "big government" programs, which helped make it exceptionally difficult for small government advocates that sought to take on the VA. William Safire wrote in the mid 1990s that "the worst big-government mistake of Ronald Reagan's was to elevate the Veterans Administration to cabinet-level."[54] While it is impossible to measure precisely the exact importance of gaining cabinet status, gaining prominence and enabling the VA to become more entrenched helped ensure that it would remain largely out of the line of fire as the debates raged in the 1990s over the size and scope of government.

Sacred Cow versus the Contract with America

The debate over raising the VA to cabinet status in some ways foreshadowed the debates over health care and welfare in the 1990s.

The 1994 congressional elections resulted in a landslide for the Republicans. The GOP gained 54 seats in the House of Representatives and 8 seats in the Senate to take control of both legislative branches. The Republicans had not controlled the House of Representatives for forty years—since 1952—and the overwhelming nature of the election was seen as giving the new Republican congressional leadership, Speaker Newt Gingrich of Georgia in the House, and Majority Leader Robert Dole of the Kansas in the Senate, a real mandate for change.

The election was seen as a repudiation of the Democratic party and its support of government social programs, especially the Clinton administration's efforts to advance First Lady Hillary Clinton's universal health care plan. The Republican Revolution sought to dismantle much of the legacy of Franklin Roosevelt's New Deal and Lyndon Johnson's Great Society programs that, in their view, were contributing to massive government deficits, high taxes, and wasteful spending, and to a society dependent on social programs and government handouts. The Republicans believed that they came into office with a mandate to reform government, and no government agency—with the notable exception of the Department of Defense—was assured of protection.

The only person standing in the way of the Republican reform agenda was President Clinton, who following the 1994 election had to shift his priorities completely. Having campaigned in 1992 on advancing universal health care and promoting other social programs, the White House was now forced to play defense with the future of New Deal and Great Society programs at stake. The stage was set for massive political battle.

The Department of Veterans Affairs had perhaps one of the most precarious positions of all. It was the newest government agency, as noted above. It was seen by many conservatives as a wasteful, bloated bureaucracy and its government-run healthcare system was completely anathema to the conservative principles of the Republican revolution. The agency was widely seen as poorly run, as there were countless cases of poor service and tremendous waste and fraud.

Additionally, the effort to create a government-run care system for the general public was crushed just before the 1994 mid-term elections. The National Center for Policy Analysis, a conservative think tank based in Dallas, called the VA health system "bloated and inefficient" and pointed out that it had a higher per person cost than any other federal medical program. The center noted that the federal government spent $5,556 per VA patient in 1992, compared with $3,790 per Medicare patient.[55] Kenneth W. Kizer, the VA's undersecretary for health, argued that if costs were higher it was due to the fact that VA patients are usually older and less healthy than patients in private hospitals.[56]

But the Department of Veterans Affairs also had some advantages that other agencies did not. The department was a Reagan administration agency. President George H.W. Bush had said that "There is only one place for the veterans of America, in the Cabinet Room, at the table with the President."[57]

Shortly after taking office, the Clinton administration contemplated attempting a dramatic reform of the VA, but the White House decided that it was unable to fight the political inertia. The *Washington Post* reported that cuts were initially contemplated as a part of Vice President Gore's "reinvent government" task force, but advisers decided against such an effort because of President Clinton's existing problems with the veterans lobby, arising from allegations that he avoided the draft during the Vietnam War, as well as blowback against his attempt to drop the ban on gays in the military.[58]

The battle lines were soon drawn. Ideological conservatives took aim at government waste and the VA was on the target list. However, the Clinton administration saw in the VA a convenient foil to the anti-government reform efforts of Speaker Gingrich. The White House would frequently use the Veterans Administration to highlight the impact of government cuts proposed by the Republicans. The powerful veterans lobby was also opposed to any cuts and would quickly take the side of the White House if the Republican congress were to advance such a proposal. This left the Republican congress stuck. If they were to follow through on the principles that they campaigned on and that many of their supporters and ideological backers were advocating, they would risk alienating a large lobby and potentially give the White House a significant political victory.

In January 1995, Conservative columnist William Safire wrote a column in the *New York Times* attacking the Department of Veterans Affairs and calling for reform. Safire wrote that "The bloated D.V.A. employs a quarter-million people; half the males are non-veterans; 7,163 make more than $100,000 a year. Spending shot up from $23 billion in 1980 to $37 billion today, even as the aging veterans' population declined from 31 to 26 million. The D.V.A.'s 54,000 hospital beds are 23 percent unfilled." Safire advocated:

> 1. Put out to pasture the sacred cow known as Veterans Affairs. Rent its fancy office space to private insurance companies. 2. End benefits for non-service-related injuries and illnesses. Privatize veterans' hospitals and offer free insurance to disabled veterans. 3. Reveal O.M.B.'s secret—that D.V.A. nursing-home care costs more than at a comparable privately run home—and give indigent veterans vouchers to grow old in dignity. Time for a new lobby: Veterans Against Special Treatment (VAST). Most of us taxpaying vets are ready to join.[59]

His column put forth the fundamental principles of American conservatism, which included a significant skepticism about the efficiency and efficacy of any government bureaucracy—especially government-run social programs, and a belief that the private sector was better suited for many of the jobs being done by federal agencies. Writing as the new Republican Congress took office, Safire was picking a fight. The Republican Party had three months earlier dramatically won back power in the House and the Senate on a platform that pledged to balance the federal budget by attacking wasteful government spending, especially entitlement and social programs like welfare and Medicaid. Safire was firing a shot at a bureaucracy that appeared very similar to those that Newt Gingrich and the GOP campaigned against.

But in writing his column, Safire was going up against a very powerful lobby and constituency that had tremendous influence in Washington. A week later on January 19, 1995, Safire wrote in his column of the response he received.

> When you zap a sacred cow, you have to brace yourself for the ensuing mooing. The cow most sacred here is the veterans' lobby. In this space last week, the unwritable was written: "the most wasteful special-interest spending in Washington" was the $37 billion to provide mediocre government medicine to veterans. The night before the column appeared, I ran into Representative Gerry Solomon, the

laudably tight-fisted new chairman of the House Rules Committee. When I told him the worst big-government mistake of Ronald Reagan's was to elevate the Veterans Administration to cabinet-level, Solomon replied cheerily that he wrote that bill and sold the President on it. Obviously the vets' lobby is not going to get money-saving heat from the Gingrich crowd.

The Legion reacted to my modest proposal by attacking a straw man: "Don't Begrudge Veterans Medical Care" was the demagogic headline over its letter to The Times. But the new idea is to privatize the present system of socialized medicine, giving disabled veterans vouchers to buy insurance for private medical care that treats them with dignity...Then Mike McCurry, the President's new press secretary, called to introduce himself and say a letter was coming from chief of staff Leon Panetta. That Clintonite seized this as a heaven-sent opportunity to pull out all the heartstops, from a treacly "the country has a sacred trust," which nobody denies, to a fear-mongering characterization of vouchers for improved private care as "the destruction of this system of support for our veterans."[60]

When Gingrich unveiled his budget proposals that January, he proposed that congress cut spending on housing by 20 percent and on the environment by more than 20 percent, but he did not propose cuts for the Veterans Administration.[61] The House and Senate sought to revamp Medicare, with Gingrich saying "We are going to rethink Medicare from the ground up," and arguing that Medicare in its current form was a "centralized bureaucratic structure offering one menu for everybody in a monopolistic manner is the opposite of how America works."[62] But the VA avoided similar scrutiny. The *Washington Times* however did quote Gingrich, saying that "Once the Republican-led Congress tackles Medicare, hospitals run by the Veteran's Administration could be the next target."[63] But Gingrich's mention of the VA was reflective of initial exuberance, not of political reality.

The Clinton administration and the Gingrich-led conservative Congress would engage in an intense political battle over the next year and one of the key arguments the Clinton administration made was to push back on veterans benefits. When the Democrats lost control of the House of Representatives in 1994, one of the most influential figures on veterans' issues, Congressman Sonny "Mr. Veteran" Montgomery of Mississippi, lost his chairmanship of the House Veterans Affairs Committee. Bill McAllister wrote at the time that:

> When it came to issues affecting the nation's 26 million veterans, Montgomery, 74, a retired major general in the Mississippi National Guard, unquestionably was the most influential person in Congress.

As chairman of the House Veterans Affairs Committee, Montgomery effectively ruled the Department of Veterans Affairs and its predecessor, the Veterans Administration, with a firm hand. While the Senate veterans' panel changed chairmen repeatedly, Montgomery was a constant, telling Cabinet secretaries what they could—and could not—do. He decided when the government would approve what benefits for veterans and, thanks to an unusual agreement with the Rules Committee, no veterans bill was subject to amendment on the House floor. That gave Montgomery power few House committee chairmen shared. But this month's elections will sweep the southern patriarch from the chairmanship, forcing VA officials, for the first time since 1981, to deal in a world without the soft-spoken Montgomery in charge.[64]

The Clinton administration used the transfer of power to stoke fears of cuts from a new Republican majority. Newt Gingrich pledged not to eliminate the House committees dealing with veterans, as they planned to do to other House committees. The Clinton administration's Secretary for the Department of Veterans' Affairs, Jesse Brown, in campaigning against GOP House candidates in the 1994 congressional election, had argued that the GOP's "Contract with America" would force deep cuts in veterans programs.

Brown argued during the campaign that the cuts envisioned by the contract amounted to $800 billion from domestic programs over five years. That, he said, would translate into a 20 percent "across-the-board reduction in VA programs ranging from medical care to compensation for disabled veterans."[65]

Republican Rep. Bob Stump of Arizona, who was tapped to replace Montgomery, said he was infuriated by Secretary Brown's comments and "resented them very much." Stump promised that the new GOP congress would not go after veterans programs and pledged continuity, saying that Secretary Brown's comments were "not true." Stump said, "We've taken our share of [budget] hits, more than our share . . . Nobody is going to go out and start cutting the programs." But a VA spokesman for Secretary Brown responded by saying "the numbers speak for themselves . . . This contract makes me very nervous. You tell me how they are going to reduce taxes, increase defense spending, balance the budget and not touch Social Security without going after domestic programs—and that includes veterans."[66]

As Clinton and Gingrich moved closer to stalemate over the budget, which would eventually result in a government shutdown, Clinton pointed to his support of veterans during his time in office. As one editorial writer noted on Veterans Day in 1995, the first day of the congressional shutdown:

> Though veterans have criticized his avoiding of the draft in the Vietnam War and his policy to allow gays to serve in the military, they have been grateful for his work on their behalf since becoming president. Mr. Clinton started the day by inviting 250 veterans and active service personnel to the White House Blue Room for breakfast. Guests included military chiefs and leaders of veteran service organizations as well as local Gulf War veterans. At Arlington National Cemetery, he told a crowd of 3500 people, including veterans in wheelchairs, that even as the size of the US government was shrinking, "the percentage of permanent jobs in the government going to our veterans has grown" since he took office in early 1993. And he said even as Washington works to cut government spending, he has sought more than a $1.4 billion increase in health care funding for the Veterans Administration. "We must rally the resources for veterans' benefits," he said.[67]

At a press conference on day three of the government shutdown, President Clinton said that he would reopen Social Security and Veterans Administration offices, because "the elderly and vets deserve better."[68]

The media often wrote stories highlighting the plight of veterans during the government shutdown. The *New York Times* quoted a pharmacist, Terrill G. Washington, who worked at the VA hospital in Washington DC: "We are here working to take care of veterans...Members of Congress went home to be with their families. They have the audacity to tell us they'll be back at the table on Friday to resume the talks. A lot of people here need their paychecks to pay for rent, food or child care."[69] Gingrich said that the Republican budget plan was "only painful for those who believe the Washington bureaucracy is the only answer."[70] But as Howard Troxler wrote in the *St. Petersburg Times,* the Democrats began using the Republican playbook:

> Some Democrats have resorted to an old Republican trick—whipping up the folks back home. They are producing all kinds of statistics about exactly how many dollars the Republican plan would cost you, even though the Republicans themselves haven't made any specific proposals. To help out, the Veterans' Administration announced this week that the Republican budget would force the VA to close one out of five of its hospitals.[71]

While the White House and congressional Democrats were using the VA to create public anxiety over the proposals of the GOP Congress, the

Democrats' arguments were bolstered by statements from some prominent conservatives and conservative institutions.

The most notable proposal came from the Heritage Foundation in April 1995. The conservative think tank, located just a few steps from the Capitol, released a report advocating the elimination of 9 of the 14 federal agencies, including the Department of Veterans Affairs, which it advocated be merged into the Department of Defense. Heritage argued the proposed cuts would save $887 billion and would help balance the budget and would enable sharp tax cuts. The report was a 260-page proposal, entitled "Rolling Back Government: A Budget Plan to Rebuild America," which drew heavily on past ideas the conservative think tank had developed over the years, especially during the Reagan Revolution.

The conservative *Washington Times* described the Heritage proposal as "one of the most ambitious downsizing blueprints to emerge thus far" and they noted that "the purpose of the plan is to show the way for timid Republicans who may still be clinging to old ways." Stuart M. Butler, the Heritage vice president for domestic policy who wrote the budget plan, said: "We want to force people to face up to the choices," acknowledging that his plan will cause much "yelling, screaming and gnashing of teeth" among interest groups in Washington."[72] Butler noted that they "we're on the edge of the mainstream now," but that in light of the defeat of Clinton's health care proposal "people are talking the same language. It's a radically changed environment" with even the most entrenched interest groups less fearful of change."[73] Butler explained that "Now, though, with the arrival of the Republican Congress, the momentum's come back to us...the 'Contract with America' [was] an important step...[but] we see it as transitional." Butler added "We're way out in front now...a lot of the things we proposed six months or a year ago—like block-granting the welfare system—have already become part of the national debate."[74]

When Heritage released the report, the *Washington Post's* Guy Gugliotta wrote that Heritage was "one of the nation's bastions of conservative thought," and their report was "certain to capture the ear of every Republican in town and boost Heritage's efforts to become the leading voice of the new Congress." Stuart Butler had said that Heritage was trying "to push the envelope while staying within the envelope...We are trying to plot a clear path to where we think things ought to go." The *Washington Post* added that "Heritage's envelope is the GOP Congress, where large numbers of eager newcomers are reaching out to conservative think tanks for expertise in budget balancing, government shrinking, restructuring and streamlining."[75]

Nationally syndicated conservative columnist Donald Lambro wrote:

> Heritage's proposed restructuring of the government, much of which operates as it did more than a century ago, should be read by every member of Congress. As GOP leaders prepare to tackle the budget next month, the worst mistake they can make is one of timidity... With $5 trillion in federal debt looming in 1996, this is a time that calls for boldness and daring. The GOP's task forces are moving in the right direction but seem too limited in their goals. Heritage's innovative plan should help to expand their field of vision.[76]

But the inclusion of the Department of Veterans Affairs in the list of nine agencies was more aspirational than a realistic assessment of what the Heritage Foundation believed could be achieved. A month after Heritage released their report, Stuart Butler admitted that they did not take on the VA, despite its large payroll and health care system, because "there is absolutely no support on the Hill." Nor should there be, argued VA Secretary Jesse Brown, who insisted that those supportive of the VA system have "the moral high ground... We have God on our side."[77] The veterans groups were also very active. Bill McAllister in a thorough article on the front page of the Sunday *Washington Post* argued that the VA was impervious to budget cuts even in cases where some were called for.

> The rest of the cash-strapped federal government may be in bureaucratic retreat... [but] the VA marches on, all but immune to the budget pressures that have forced other agencies to offer buyouts, cut services and in some cases fight for their very existence... Why is no secret: Veterans have almost unmatched political clout. Their strength cannot be fully explained either by numbers or by grassroots organization, although veterans groups rightly boast of both. More than that, it is an ethos, a deep-rooted belief that veterans have sacrificed in their country's service... Perhaps unique among federal agencies, the department stirs the hearts of flag-waving conservatives, who support its patriotic purpose, and hard-core liberals, who know its programs largely serve a lower income population. Few other programs are so sacrosanct and so routinely defy budget cutters' attacks on waste.[78]

Conservative think tanks also adopted a piecemeal critique of the Department of Veterans Affairs. The Heritage Foundation issued reports that advocated reform of the agency, as well as calling for its abolition. A Heritage "Backgrounder" in the Summer of 1990 that assessed growing government debt had a section devoted to the VA, but focused just on the VA's mortgage loan program. The Heritage paper argued that the mortgage program was making risky loans and was turning into a blanket entitlement program. It noted that:

> Because the program was established to reward veterans for their service and was not meant to be financially self-sufficient, a reform of the program should aim at bringing the taxpayer liability under control, not at an eventual elimination of taxpayer exposure. To accomplish this package of reforms a thorough review should be undertaken of the VA's underwriting standards to determine whether too many risky borrowers are using the program. The program was never meant to be a blanket entitlement for all veterans, only those who could demonstrate an ability to repay the loan were deemed qualified for a VA guaranteed mortgage.[79]

The Heritage backgrounder sought to limit the mortgage program's scope and to hold the line on the VA's activities. Similarly, in March 1995, Heritage released a backgrounder on the need for the use of more private sector contractors.

> Despite their reputation for poor service, however, the staff and management of Veterans Administration hospitals have been protected from competition by a variety of federal laws and regulations. Until recently, for example, legislation established an employment floor of 157,000 for total VA personnel, so using outside management personnel would have forced the VA to add rather than reduce hospital staff. Other laws explicitly prohibit the contracting out of activities of the Department of Medicine and Surgery. And while the government workforce is given a 10 percent cost preference in all other federal contracting, in [the] VA that preference was 15 percent, and the private bidder was required to add the government's review costs to his own when submitting the bid, until 1994 when Congress, recognizing the excessive costs these restrictions imposed on veterans' programs, agreed to place these restrictions in abeyance for five years.[80]

Conservative arguments advocating piecemeal reform could be justified as an effort to enhance the efficiency of the VA. This more limited approach, while still difficult, had a greater chance of being implemented. Similarly, House and Senate budget committees at the time took moderate stands against increasing VA spending and even proposed mild cuts that were in stark contrast to the approach that House members advocated for other government agencies.[81]

In the end, the Department of Veterans Affairs survived the 1995 government shutdown and the ideological showdown with little trouble. The Democrats also found in the VA an issue that proved a convenient foil against conservative arguments on spending, as well as on national security.

Veterans and Presidential Politics

Unlike in most previous elections, support for veterans' benefits has become a major issue in each of the last four presidential elections and has been used by the candidates to attack their political opponents. Injecting veterans' issues into a presidential campaign has tremendous importance. Turning support for veterans into a political issue forces candidates to defend their past record and often forces each candidate to make commitments and pledges to maintain or increase funding for the nation's veterans. No candidate for presidential office wants to risk alienating or angering such a large and influential voting bloc.

1996 Presidential Campaign

In 1996, President Clinton was running for re-election against a wounded World War II veteran, Senator Bob Dole of Kansas. The election came on the heels of the government shutdown and the fight between the White House and Congress over how to balance the budget. The conservative Congress advocated aggressive spending cuts to balance the budget and the White House resisted. During the 1996 campaign, the Clinton-Gore campaign repeatedly attacked the Dole campaign on veterans' issues, arguing that Dole's pledges to cut spending and to balance the budget would require significant cuts in veterans' benefits.

Vice President Al Gore spoke at the Veterans of Foreign Wars and argued that the Veterans Administration would be on a list of government agencies that would be under the knife to pay for Senator Dole's proposed $548 billion tax cut. Gore told the audience that "with the Republican plan, veterans would have to pay. There is no way around it."[82]

In the same speech Gore sought to contrast the Republican Congress's record on veterans with the Clinton administration's. Gore argued that in 1995 President Clinton had twice vetoed the budget passed by the Republican-controlled congress that he said would have cut benefits for veterans, adding that "now they're up to the same old tricks with even bigger tax cuts, even more indiscriminate, and they have absolutely no way to pay for it." Gore asked the audience of veterans to note that Clinton sought to increase veterans benefits by $1 billion, but that the GOP-controlled Congress cut that budget request by more than 90 percent or $915 million.[83]

Dole spoke before Gore at the VFW and attempted to preempt Gore's attacks saying that he would not balance the budget "on the back of America's veterans."[84] But a few weeks later Dole was put on the defensive campaigning in the South. In Georgia he was asked by a woman who had heard talk that to pay for tax cuts Dole was going to have to cut veterans benefits. Dole responded abruptly, "It's not going to happen in a Dole administration... Nobody is going to touch those benefits and don't listen to all the Clinton people."[85]

Attacking Dole's proposals as bad for veterans served to help blunt the political impact of Dole's military service and accusations that Clinton avoided the draft. Showing support for veterans' issues can help political leaders that lack military service in races against candidates with significant military backgrounds.

2000 Presidential Campaign

During the 2000 presidential campaign, neither candidate had a substantial military record. Vice President Al Gore had served in Vietnam as a military reporter, which gave him an advantage over then-Governor George W. Bush's spotty service in the Air National Guard, which had drawn scrutiny.

Moreover, by 2000 the momentum behind the Republican revolution had dissipated. The Republican Congress had lost much of the mandate it had acquired in 1994; its leadership had been decimated. The Democrats had actually gained seats in the 1998 congressional election, and President Clinton was leaving office with high approval ratings. George W. Bush campaigned as a "compassionate conservative," by which he sought to paint himself as a conservative with a softer edge who cared about people and about social issues like improving education. It was a clear effort to distance Bush from former Speaker Gingrich and the public's perception of him as uncaring. While in 1994 it might have been at least conceivable for a politician to run against government waste and attack the Veterans Administration—even though few attempted this at the time—by 2000 the mood had shifted and Bush actually attacked the Clinton administration for not doing enough for veterans. Additionally, the deficits that seemed so intractable in 1994 and that the Republican congress had rallied against had disappeared. By 2000, the federal government was actually running a budget surplus, making the big debate of 2000 what to do with that extra money. Budget cutting was off the table.

Governor Bush attacked Gore (as the *New York Times* described it) by telling "the veterans that if he is elected president, he will make it a priority to ensure that veterans get the benefits they were promised without the bureaucratic delays that he said were too prevalent today. To that end, he said he would create what he called a 'veterans health care task force.'"

Bush said "In my administration, the Department of Veterans Affairs will act as an advocate for veterans seeking benefits and claims, not act as an adversary."[86] Bush pledged to "streamline the disability-claims process for veterans and assemble a task force to improve their health care."[87] Advocating the creation of a task force and pledging to run an organization more efficiently was hardly a controversial approach.

In a speech to the VFW, Bush pledged to increase military pay by $1 billion per year, increase VA health care services, and to spend more to improve schools that serve military children. The *Philadelphia Inquirer* noted that "Several thousand VFW members and their relatives rewarded Bush with a standing ovation."[88]

Doug Hattaway, a Gore spokesman, responded to Bush's speech, arguing that Bush was making promises he could not keep, "By using up the entire [federal budget] surplus on a tax cut for the rich, he leaves nothing to invest in military pay or readiness."[89] In a speech to the VFW, Gore promised that, if elected, he would increase spending on veterans' education by $1.2 billion over five years—the largest increase since World War II. Gore attacked Bush's proposed tax cuts, saying that they were targeted to help the wealthy "at the expense of everyone else" and would "wreck our good economy and make it impossible to modernize our armed forces, meet our commitments to veterans and keep [the military] ready for battle." Gore challenged Bush's proposed spending on the military and veterans, "Where is the [money] coming from? Will it come from the trust fund? If so, the trust fund would go bankrupt quickly. Would it come from general revenue? If so, the entire budget would go quickly into very deep deficits again, ending the prosperity. Would it come from tax increases? Would it come from benefit cuts? Those are the only four places it could come from that I can see. Now, if they've got another possibility, they really should spell that out."[90] It was a familiar argument, and closely resembled the one used by Clinton against Dole in 1996 and by Democrats against the Republicans following 1994.

Bush's pledge to increase spending on veterans benefits demonstrated that despite the traditional conservative opposition to social welfare benefit programs, veterans benefits, like social security, proved too politically popular to take on and conversely offered significant political opportunities. Bush won a narrow Electoral College victory with significant support in key states with military communities, including the majority of the nation's veterans.

2004 Presidential Campaign
With the election of George W. Bush in 2000, the Republican party controlled the entire legislative branch (House and Senate) and the executive

branch, but the conservative movement did not have the same force of popularity that it had had in 1994. The Republicans had lost seats in the House each successive election and lost control of the Senate when Senator Jim Jeffords of Vermont switched parties from Republican to Independent.

The 2004 presidential election pitted a decorated Vietnam veteran against a wartime president whose reelection campaign argued that as president he was the best person to keep America safe. Additionally, in the aftermath of the 9/11 terrorist attacks, the political debate became highly charged and showing one's patriotism was seen as essential, as was vividly demonstrated by Senator Kerry's salute and opening line at his speech at the Democratic Convention, "I'm John Kerry, and I'm reporting for duty." After 9/11, demonstrating one's support on veterans' issues had greater political significance than ever before.

Following the attacks on 9/11 and the subsequent wars in Afghanistan and Iraq, increasing strain was placed on the VA system, as more and more veterans returned home needing care. The Bush administration did not anticipate protracted conflicts in either Afghanistan or Iraq, as projections within the Pentagon at the onset of the Iraq war assumed that a significant drawdown of troops would happen in the first few months following the invasion. When each war began to take a much greater toll on the men and women of the armed forces than was anticipated before the wars, the administration and the VA were caught off-guard. Additionally, the costs of medical care had skyrocketed across the board, creating even more strain on the VA's budgets. Yet in 2004, the full measure of the problems afflicting the VA were not yet completely apparent, as the United States had been in Iraq for little more than a year. The full scope of the challenges afflicting the U.S. system for caring for the veterans of the wars in Iraq and Afghanistan, particularly the wounded veterans, was not fully realized until after the election, most notably with the Walter Reed scandal in 2007. While Walter Reed is a DoD facility and not a VA facility, the failings there made it vividly clear to the country that more needed to be done to take care of returning service members.

Early in the summer of 2004, Democrats in the Senate sought to demonstrate their support for veterans by proposing to increase spending on veterans health care by 30 percent and mandating future increases that would be indexed to the number of veterans and to national health care costs. President Bush's campaign was critical of the effort, arguing that spending on health care for veterans had increased by 40 percent under their administration. Steve Schmidt, a Bush campaign spokesman, and the future campaign manager for John McCain in 2008, said that "Mandatory spending increases are the wrong approach for America's veterans."[91] *Boston Globe* columnist Tom Oliphant wrote at the time

> What was being proposed—by Democratic Leader Tom Daschle of South Dakota—was a change that would make health care for veterans like Social Security or Medicare: If you're eligible, you get treated. In government-speak, it's called an entitlement. Instead of keeping a promise made to people who earned it the hard way, the government makes its promise subject to the annual whims of administration budgeters and congressional appropriators... The problem, however, is not cost estimates, it is what Bush has done to the hemorrhaging federal budget. There will never be any room for closing the gap between supply and demand in veterans' health care as long as Bush's priorities hold. As a practical matter, keeping the top marginal income tax rate at 36 percent and completely eliminating inheritance taxes on multi-million-dollar estates means there is no room for veterans. Last week's vote never had a chance... A point was made, however, and it registered clearly with the Partnership for Veterans Health Care Benefit Reform, which includes every veterans organization there is. Kerry is for it. Bush is against it. Simple as that, and playing games with the Senate's schedule won't change the reality.[92]

The Kerry campaign pledged to improve veterans health care, as well as other benefits and accused the Bush administration of neglecting those who served.[93] Kerry said at a Democratic presidential primary debate in January 2004 that, "This president is breaking faith with veterans all across the country... They've cut the VA budget by $1.8 billion."[94] This attack was premised on the notion that while the Bush administration had increased funding in some respects, but the funding increases were deemed deficient by many veterans groups, as well as the Democrats in congress. During the 2004 victory, the *Boston Globe* noted, "Bush has never cut the agency's budget—at least not in the conventional sense of the word. The president has proposed increasing its discretionary budget—funding for programs not required by law—in each of his annual budget proposals."[95] But this increase was seen as paltry by veterans groups that complained the department needed a billion in additional funding. Bush's own Secretary of Veterans Affairs, Anthony J. Principi, even suggested that his agency was underfunded, telling congress in February 2007 that "I asked OMB [the Office of Management and Budget] for $1.2 billion more than I received,"[96] Democrats also pointed out that the increases in the VA's discretionary spending amounted to a cut since the increases proposed by Bush would not allow them to continue services at the same level, because of the impact of the wars in Iraq and Afghanistan and the increase in health care costs.[97]

The Kerry campaign also attacked the Bush administration for increasing veterans health care costs by mandating additional fees, from an annual fee for some and increasing the drug co-payment. Senator Kerry warned that as a result of policies of the Bush administration, 200,000 veterans would be driven from health care.[98] Kerry also attacked Bush for not living up to his promises to improve the efficiency of the VA health care system, saying at a campaign rally that Bush "refuses to lift a finger to help the quarter of a million veterans who've waited half a year just to see a doctor for the first time."[99]

2008 Presidential Campaign

The 2008 election saw John McCain, a career naval officer, highly esteemed Vietnam veteran, and former prisoner of war who was widely viewed as a war hero, face Barack Obama, a much younger presidential candidate. As the first candidate of the post-Vietnam generation, which did not have to deal with the draft. Senator Obama, unlike McCain, had not served in the military. However, Senator McCain's record on supporting the expansion of veterans benefits was considered poor by many and he was subsequently attacked throughout the campaign for his inconsistency.

Senator Obama repeatedly lavished praise on McCain's war record and would describe McCain as a war hero. But the Obama campaign aggressively critiqued McCain's stance on veterans' issues. McCain responded forcefully in response to one such attack. The AP noted that "Republican John McCain said Thursday that Democrat Barack Obama had no right to criticize McCain's position on military scholarships because the Illinois senator did not serve in uniform. 'And I will not accept from Senator Obama, who did not feel it was his responsibility to serve our country in uniform, any lectures on my regard for those who did,' the Arizona senator said in a harshly worded statement."[100]

But liberal advocates of Senator Obama pointed out that in his time in the Senate, Obama had consistently supported veterans health and education benefits and was a cosponsor of the 21st-century GI Bill that put veterans benefits on par with those provided after World War II, while McCain, on the other hand, had a spotty record on veterans' issues and had had received relatively poor ratings from some prominent veterans groups. Moreover, he also did not support and did not show up to vote for the 21st century GI Bill.

McCain's record on veterans affairs provided a treasure trove of material for Obama to counterattack and numerous progressive veterans groups were quick to contrast their records. Senator Obama was aided by possessing a less lengthy record, but used his votes in the Senate to demonstrate his support for veterans' issues. But McCain was attacked on his lengthy legislative history that extended back into the 1980s. According to Project VetVoice, the blog of the progressive veterans group VoteVets, "since arriving in the U.S. Senate in 1987, McCain has voted at least 28 times against ensuring important benefits for America's veterans, including providing adequate healthcare." It was pointed out that McCain on numerous occasions, such as in 1995, 1996, 2000, 2001, 2003 and 2006, voted either in opposition to increased funding for the Department of Veterans Affairs, or in support of measures that cut veterans funding. Progressive national security groups used these votes as evidence that McCain's claims that he will "take care of them (veterans)," was at odds with his record.[101] McCain was asked at one of his campaign town hall meetings by an audience member to explain his votes against funding veterans measures. McCain's inability to explain these votes adequately was jumped on by his political opponents and used to demonstrate that McCain had a poor record on veterans' issues.[102]

Veterans groups played a significant role during the election. The nonpartisan Disabled American Veterans gave Senator McCain a 20 percent rating for his voting record on veterans' issues.[103] Similarly, the nonpartisan Iraq and Afghanistan Veterans of America gave McCain a "D" grade for his poor voting record on veterans' issues, including his votes against additional body armor for troops in combat and additional funding for PTSD and TBI screening and treatment.[104] These groups noted that McCain had also repeatedly voted against increasing funding for veterans health care and veterans benefits. On the other hand, Senator Obama received an 80 percent rating from Disabled American Veterans and received a "B" grade from IAVA.[105] Veterans for America also criticized Republican vice presidential candidate Governor Sarah Palin's performance in dealing with veterans returning from Afghanistan and Iraq, saying "as a result of inadequate leadership from the Governor of Alaska, among others, the Alaska National Guard has an inadequate understanding of the full range of post-combat issues facing those who have served abroad from the Alaska Guard in recent years."

A major area of disagreement between the candidates was over the introduction of the 21st-century GI Bill. Not surprisingly, both candidates had poor attendance records in the Senate during the campaign, McCain missed six of the nine votes on veterans' issues and Obama missed four. But during the summer, Senator Obama made a point to attend the senate and vote on the new 21st-century GI Bill, in which he was a cosponsor. Senator McCain opposed the bill and missed the vote to attend a fundraiser. The liberal website Talking Points Memo wrote that "The Senate just voted to pass Jim Webb's 21st Century version of the G.I. bill, which would greatly expand educational benefits to veterans. Guess who skipped it? John McCain. McCain, who touts his support for veterans, had previously declined to support the bill...And rather than vote against it, he skipped the vote instead."[106]

The GI Bill was popular throughout the country. The *Sarasota Herald Tribune* wrote, "Yesterday the U.S. Senate approved modernizing the GI Bill for many good reasons...The proposed GI Bill benefits are hardly lavish, in light of the demands on today's military and the cost of living facing today's veterans, who are often older than vets in the past and married with children. The bill approved by the Senate would, essentially, place the benefits on par with those once granted to World War II vets—and, wisely, extend them to active reservists and the National Guard...The opposition's argument fails on numerous counts...The veterans who would qualify for the modernized benefits—those who have served in the military for at least three years since Sept. 11, 2001—deserve them. Yes, they deserve them." This is just one of the reasons that Iraq and Afghanistan Veterans for America gave John McCain a "D" on their congressional report card.[107]

Like 1996 and 2004, the 2008 election demonstrated that even a candidate with a seemingly heroic military record could be attacked on veterans' issues if his records was not completely in line with the veterans lobby.

Conclusion

As a result of the downsizing of the military after the war in Vietnam and the end of the Cold War, the veterans' population is shrinking. Some 900 World War II veterans die every day and about 40 percent of all veterans are over the age of 65. Not only does caring for such a large aging population have considerable costs, but it may also have potentially adverse implications for the political clout of veterans, as the population of veterans declines. Yet if anything the political influence of veterans seems to have grown over the last decade. Much of this is due to the wars in Afghanistan and Iraq, the politicization of patriotism, and the decline of veterans in Congress. Both Afghanistan and Iraq are the first protracted wars to be fought by an all-volunteer military, which has put tremendous strain on those who volunteered to serve. This has created an intense feeling of obligation throughout the country, and especially among those political leaders who have not served in the military, to demonstrate support for men and women in the military. One way to do this is through supporting veterans benefits.

Nevertheless, the political clout of veterans has not meant that the Department of Veterans Affairs is without problems. While funding has increased, the VA system has been placed under tremendous strain by the protracted conflicts. It has often been criticized for poor performance and inefficiencies. In some respect, inefficiencies and poor management are an inherent trait of very large bureaucracies. But many of the problems in the VA are also reflective of a governing philosophy that holds government benefit and entitlement programs in disdain. While the Bush administration marginally increased the budget of the Department of Veterans Affairs, the VA's problems were compounded during the Bush administration because it was managed and run by those who believe that government is often part of the problem. This frequently led them to take a more hands off approach. This will be discussed in greater detail in the next three chapters.

Notes

1. Alec Campbell, "The Invisible Welfare State: Establishing the Phenomenon of Twentieth Century Veteran's Benefits," *Journal of Political and Military Sociology* 32, no. 2 (2004): 250.

2. Department of Veterans Affairs, "A Brief History of the VA." http://www.va.gov/facmgt/historic/Brief_VA_History.asp.

3. Department of Veterans Affairs, "2008 VA Organizational Briefing Book," May 2008. http://www.va.gov/ofcadmin/docs/vaorgbb.pdf.

4. Ibid.

5. Congressional Research Service, "Veterans Affairs: Historical Budget Authority, Fiscal Years 1940 through 2007," June 13, 2008. http://fas.org/sgp/crs/misc/RS22897.pdf.

6. Campbell, "The Invisible Welfare State," 250.

7. Ibid., 253.

8. Bill McAllister, "VA Hospitals Impervious to Budget Knife; Treating Fewer Patients, VA Hospitals Defy Gravity of Budget Cuts," *Washington Post,* May 21, 1995.

9. Charles Stratford, "Reagan's Plan for Veterans is FUBAR," *St. Petersburg Times,* November 22, 1987.

10. American Legion Web site, http://www.legion.org/homepage.php.

11. Veterans of Foreign Wars Web site, http://www.vfw.org/index.cfm?fa=news.levelc&cid=223&tok=1.

12. Ibid.

13. Ibid.

14. Ryan Bender, "VFW, American Legion Back Iraq War—Groups Urge Patience to Let 'Surge' Work," *Boston Globe,* August 16, 2007.

15. Ibid.

16. Iraq and Afghanistan Veterans of America, "Annual Report; Fiscal Year 2007," http://iava.org/documents/IAVA2007AnnualReport.pdf.

17. Ibid.

18. Veterans for America Web site, http://www.veteransforamerica.org/about/.

19. Ibid.

20. VoteVets Web site, www.votevets.org.

21. Vets for Freedom Web site, www.vetsforfreedom.org.

22. Vets for Freedom, "Vets for Freedom Supports Revised GI Bill," Press Release, May 14, 2008, http://www.vetsforfreedom.org/presscenter/blogitem. aspx?id=433.

23. McAllister, "VA Hospitals Impervious to Budget Knife."

24. Campbell, "The Invisible Welfare State," 253.

25. Associated Press, "Reagan Would Elevate V.A. to Cabinet Level," *New York Times,* November 11, 1987.

26. Ibid.

27. Peter Grier, "Thursday VA's Cabinet Status Is Slow in Coming," *Christian Science Monitor,* December 17, 1987.

28. Editorial, "Senators Fear Politicization of the VA; Plan for Cabinet-Level Status Would Add Political Appointees," *Washington Post,* December 10, 1987.

29. *The Economist,* "Vets Dept," November 21, 1987.

30. Associated Press, "Reagan Would Elevate V.A. to Cabinet Level."

31. Tom Kenworthy, "House Votes To Give VA Cabinet Status," *Washington Post,* October 7, 1988.

32. Ibid.

33. Editorial, "Senators Fear Politicization of the VA."

34. Associated Press, "Reagan Would Elevate V.A. to Cabinet Level."

35. Editorial, "How to Remember the Cabinet," *New York Times,* October 20, 1988.

36. Editorial, "A Bulging Cabinet," *New York Times,* January, 5, 1988.

37. Tom Kenworthy, "House Votes To Give VA Cabinet Status," *Washington Post,* October 7, 1988.

38. Associated Press, "Reagan Would Elevate V.A. to Cabinet Level."

39. Ibid.

40. Grier, "Thursday VA's Cabinet Status Is Slow in Coming."

41. Bill McAllister, "Elevating the VA: Are There Benefits?; Studies Strengthen Doubts on Granting Cabinet Status; Judicial Review of Claims Sought," *Washington Post,* March 16, 1988.

42. Ibid.

43. William Safire, "The End of the Affair," *New York Times,* November 29, 1987.

44. "Senators Fear Politicization of the VA; Plan for Cabinet-Level Status Would Add Political Appointees," *Washington Post,* December 10, 1987.

45. Grier, "Thursday VA's Cabinet Status Is Slow in Coming."

46. Editorial, "Veterans Stampede Congress," *New York Times,* December 14, 1987.

47. "Veterans Department Legislation Signed," *Washinton Post,* October 26, 1988.

48. "Vet Clout," *Christian Science Monitor,* November 18, 1987.

49. Charles Stafford, "Reagan's Plan for Veterans is FUBAR," *St. Petersburg Times,* November 22, 1987

50. "Senators Fear Politicization of the VA."

51. Ibid.

52. Editorial, "How to Remember the Cabinet," *New York Times,* October 20, 1988.

53. Brian Faler, "Doing the Cabinet Shuffle; Experts Debate Homeland Plan's Rank Among Reorganizations," *Washington Post,* July 31, 2002.

54. William Safire, "Sacred Cow, II," *New York Times,* January 19, 1995.

55. McAllister, "VA Hospitals Impervious to Budget Knife."

56. Ibid.

57. William Safire, "Sacred Cow," *New York Times,* January 12, 1995.

58. McAllister, "VA Hospitals Impervious to Budget Knife."

59. Safire, "Sacred Cow."

60. Saffire, "Sacred Cow, II."

61. John King, "Gingrich: GOP Won't Bend on Budget Some Areas Are Non-negotiable, He Said. He Accused Democrats of "Tawdry," Misleading Attacks," Associated Press, November 22, 1995.

62. Karen Riley, "Medicare Target of Congress' Checkup," *Washington Times,* January 31, 1995.

63. Ibid.

64. Bill McAllister, "Program Continuity Pledged as 'Mr. Veteran' Steps Down," *Washington Post,* November 17, 1994.

65. Ibid.

66. Ibid.

67. S. Holland, "Clinton Woos Veterans," *Sun Herald,* November 13, 1995.

68. Ceci Connolly, "No Relief Is in Sight for Shutdown," *St. Petersburg Times,* November 17, 1995.

69. Jerry Gray, "Aides for 2 Sides Renew the Quest for a Dudget Deal," *New York Times,* December 28, 1995.

70. Howard Troxler, "Congress Needs More than Good Intentions," *St. Peterburg Times,* May 19, 1995.

71. Ibid.

72. Patrice Hill, "Government Discovers Less Is More: Downsizing Plans Are All Bbusiness," *Washington Times,* April 18, 1995.

73. Ibid.

74. Guy Gugliotta, "A Bold 'Budget Plan to Rebuild America'; Heritage Foundation Wants to Set GOP's Course," *Washington Post,* April 17, 1995.

75. Ibid.

76. Donald Lambro, "The Dynamics of Dismantling," *Washington Times,* April 20, 1995.

77. McAllister, "VA Hospitals Impervious to Budget Knife."

78. Ibid.

79. Ronald Utt, "The Six Trillion Dollar Debt Iceberg; A Review of the Government's Risk Exposure," Heritage Foundation Backgrounder, No. 774, June 28, 1990.

80. Ronald D. Utt, "Cutting the Deficit and Improving Services By Contracting Out," Heritage Foundation Backgrounder, No. 1022, March 10, 1995.

81. McAllister, "VA Hospitals Impervious to Budget Knife."

82. Richard Sisk, "Dole Is Hit on Vets, Clinton Is Best for 'Em, Sez Gore," *Daily News* (New York), August 22, 1996.

83. Ibid.

84. Ibid.

85. Edward Walsh, "Dole Goes on Defensive In Southern Stumping," *Washington Post,* September 10, 1996.

86. Frank Bruni, "Bush Sees Military Decline And Pledges a Turnaround,"*New York Times,* August 22, 2000.

87. Dave Boyer, "Gore Forgoes Speaking to Legion Convention; First No-show by a White House Hopeful Irks Veterans," *Washington Times,* September 7, 2000.

88. Ron Hutcheson and Jodi Enda, "Bush Fires Fusillades on Abuse of Military," *Philadelphia Inquirer,* August 22, 2000.

89. Ibid.

90. Jodi Enda and Ron Hutcheson, "Gore Counters Bush on Military's Health," *Philadelphia Inquirer,* August 23, 2000.

91. James Kuhnhenn, "Kerry Returns, But Vote Delayed; He Skipped a Fundraiser to Vote on Veterans' Health Benefits, but The GOP Thwarted His Move," *Philadelphia Inquirer,* June 23, 2004.

92. Thomas Oliphant, "Broken Promises to Veterans," *Boston Globe,* June 27, 2004.

93. David Stout, "Veterans to Draw Contrasts between Kerry and Bush," *International Herald Tribune,* July 27, 2004.

94. Brian Faler, "VA Funding Dispute Not a Simple Matter; Kerry Decries Budget Cuts by Bush, but There Have Been None in Usual Sense," *Washington Post,* March 24, 2004.

95. Ibid.

96. Ibid.

97. Ibid.

98. Ibid.

99. Ibid.

100. Libby Quaid, "McCain, Obama, Spar on GI Bill," Associated Press, May 22, 2008.

101. Vet Voice, 10/01/08, http://www.vetvoice.com/showDiary.do?diaryId=1973

102. Keith Olberman, "McCain Testy Dialogue with Vet," Countdown, MSNBC, July 9, 2008, http://www.youtube.com/watch?v=zk6Q4aSiI84&eurl.

103. Disabled American Veterans, Congressional Ratings, http://www.votes mart.org/issue_rating_detail.php?r_id=3483.

104. Iraq and Afghanistan Veterans of America Action Fund, Congressional Ratings, 2006, http://www.iava.org/full-ratings-list.

105. Disabled American Veterans, Congressional Ratings.

106. Josh Marshall, "McCain Skips Vote on 21st Century GI Bill," Talking Points Memo, May 22, 2008, http://tpmelectioncentral.talkingpointsmemo.com/2008/05/breaking_mccain_skips_vote_on.php.

107. Editorial, "Troops Deserve a New GI Bill," *Sarasota Herald Tribune,* May 23, 2008.

Veteran Demographics: Today's Population, Tomorrow's Projections

Sean E. Duggan

Most Americans agree that we have no greater moral imperative than to ensure that the soldiers, sailors, airmen, coast guardsmen, and marines who have volunteered or been drafted to defend our country receive not only the best medical care and benefits our country can provide, but are also supported with programs and policies that improve their quality of life both during and after service.

However, as the debate over the future of the U.S. military presence in Iraq and Afghanistan plays out in Washington, policy makers and the American people have often lost perspective on the stress those wars have placed on the men and women of our armed services. Equally important, both lawmakers and the American public have not yet grasped the strain placed on the Department of Veterans Affairs (VA) system that is meant to support these service members and their families with the proper medical care and benefits they deserve upon their return home.

Public attention over the last seven years has understandably focused on the ability of the Department of Veterans Affairs to provide for the needs of the hundreds of thousands of Iraq and Afghanistan veterans currently entering the VA system. Less attention, however, has been paid to the agency's ability to care for the entire veteran population including the millions of veterans from previous eras who are already in the system. Together, these two populations are placing an enormous amount of stress on the VA system, a strain that will increasingly affect the ability of the VA to provide proper and timely services and benefits to all veterans seeking care.

In terms of demographics, the "current veteran population"—those veterans of previous conflicts and veterans of the wars in Iraq and Afghanistan who have already attained VA status—in the United States is shrinking, but will require a great amount of specialized care over the long-term. Today, there are over 24 million living veterans and an additional 37 million spouses, children, or other veteran dependents and survivors of deceased veterans. Together this population amounts to about 20 percent of the entire U.S. populace.[1]

This relatively older veteran population is set to be joined by large numbers of future veterans from the wars in Iraq and Afghanistan. As of the end of 2008, over 1.8 million servicemen and women have served in these theaters since 2001. While over half of these 1.8 million troops (approximately 970,000 men and women) have been discharged from military service and have entered or are entering the VA, the other half (approximately 860,000 men and women)—and the hundreds of thousands of troops that will serve in either Iraq or Afghanistan before U.S. involvement in each conflict is over—will continue to strain the VA system for decades to come.

The VA is currently struggling to meet the needs of the new wave of Iraq and Afghanistan veterans while at the same time providing for veterans from previous eras. As large numbers of veterans from both eras demand VA healthcare and benefits in increasing numbers, cracks in the VA system's capacity to care properly for all veterans in a timely fashion have already begun to appear.

While the VA's budget has increased marginally in recent years, the VA operates within a budget that competes with other government agencies and programs and is under the discretion of the Congress. As such, access to its health care services is limited by design. Consequently, the VA has been forced to limit the number of veterans it treats by implementing an eight-tiered priority ranking system, relying on waiting lists, and—advertently or not—creating a complicated bureaucratic maze of administrative impediments to veterans seeking to access VA care. While the VA is able to provide excellent health care and benefits to those veterans able to access the system, even world-class health care and generous benefits are of no use to those who cannot access them.

Despite broad recognition of the stress placed on the VA by the ongoing wars in Iraq and Afghanistan, the Bush administration did not adequately increase the VA's capacity to deal with the surge of new veterans into the system. After repeatedly assuring the armed services that "help was on the way" during the 2000 presidential campaign, the Bush administration committed our nation to two costly wars while cutting taxes. While President Bush was able to secure more than $200 billion to surge an additional five brigade combat teams into the war in Iraq in early 2007, there has not been a parallel surge in funds to care for today's service men and women upon their return home. While nearly $1 trillion has been appropriated for the wars in Iraq and Afghanistan through supplemental war funding since 2001, the Bush administration committed less than one percent of its supplemental funding to veteran care.[2]

Until Fiscal Year 2005, there were no supplemental funds appropriated for the Department of Veterans Affairs to augment its capacity to care for current veterans and the flood of incoming veterans.[3] While a lack of funding is by no means the only causal factor, it is becoming increasingly clear that the VA is unable to provide world-class health care and benefits in a timely fashion to the current veteran population and is woefully unprepared for the onslaught of future veterans from the wars in Iraq and Afghanistan that will enter the system in the coming decades.

Some policy makers have attempted to relieve the growing strain placed on the VA by significantly narrowing the pool of veteran who are eligible to obtain VA health care and other benefits. For example, "In 2003, former VA Secretary Anthony Principi announced the decision to ration care based on (veteran) need and income level. Principi suspended enrollment of the lowest veteran priority group ("priority group 8"), those who were above a certain income level and not disabled, and increased copayments and other fees for other groups." This restriction has placed VA health care out of reach for at least 400,000 veterans since 2003.[4]

Some in Congress have called for even stricter limitations. During his 2008 presidential campaign, Senator John McCain (R-AZ) called for a policy to "concentrate" veteran health care on those with combat injuries.[5] Although he did not elaborate on this plan, such a policy would have the potential to cut off VA health care to veterans who were injured while performing noncombat-related duties (e.g., service members who incurred injuries in a car accident while in Iraq or who experienced mental problems as a result of their deployments to combat zones).

Moreover, in a "little-noticed regulation change in March 2008, the military's definition of combat-related disabilities was narrowed, costing some injured veterans thousands of dollars in lost benefits." According to William J. Carr, deputy undersecretary of defense, the Pentagon narrowed the definition of a combat-related injury and argued that it "was necessary to preserve the 'special distinction for those who incur disabilities while participating in the risk of combat, in contrast with those injured otherwise.'"[6] Such views assume that the capacity of the Department of Veterans Affairs is permanently fixed, and that we should redefine the promise we made to care for our veterans upon their return home.

This is the wrong course. Americans cannot afford to disenfranchise a generation of returning veterans—as we did after Vietnam—nor can we afford to deter future generations from volunteering for military service.

If the American people are to keep the promise made to those who defend our country, the 111th Congress and a new administration must be prepared to augment the capacity of the Department of Veterans Affairs system to care for all veterans in a timely fashion regardless of when they served or in what capacity. But providing more funds to boost the VA's capacity will not be enough. The VA must recognize and rectify the administrative impediments that veterans face in accessing VA health care and benefits; at the same time they must seek to meet the specialized needs of both old and new veterans by tailoring their services to their needs.

Chapter 4 will analyze demographics and trends within the current veteran population and will assess trends in the incoming wave of Iraq and Afghanistan veterans.

Chapter 5 will assess the administrative barriers veterans face in accessing VA care and benefits. As the demands on the Department of Veterans affairs continue to increase, waiting lists, administrative bottlenecks, bureaucratic inefficiencies and claims backlogs are preventing many veterans from receiving timely VA care and benefits. While the *quality* of medical care is likely to continue to be high for those veterans able to *access* VHA services, the increased demand for those services will mean that not all facilities will be able to provide quality care in a timely manner.

Chapter 6 will provide an in-depth analysis of the multiple epidemics in veterans' mental health—Posttraumatic Stress Disorder (PTSD) and Traumatic Brain Injury (TBI) in particular.

Before examining the incoming wave of Iraq and Afghanistan veterans and their immediate and future impact on the VA care system, it is important to outline the demographics of the current veteran population.

The Overall Picture: A Shrinking Population in Need of More Care

The face of the current veteran population is rapidly changing. Overall, the current veteran population is declining both absolutely and as a percentage of the overall U.S. population as large numbers of World War II and Korea-era veterans die each year. However, large numbers of Vietnam-era veterans are aging and are seeking more services and benefits from the VA than previously anticipated. Concurrently, a parallel surge of younger veterans from Iraq and Afghanistan with severe long-term needs are entering the VA system, and will require services and benefits in unanticipated numbers.

Together, these populations are placing great stress on the VA system. As the current veteran population continues to age it will require significantly more care and benefits than the VA has demonstrated it is currently capable of providing. In order to meet the needs of today's changing veteran population, the nation's political leaders must ensure that the VA is able to address the changing needs of its beneficiaries.

As indicated in Table 4.1, currently there are over 24 million living veterans, along with 37 million dependents. Together, these 61 million people represent approximately 20 percent of the total U.S. population. While the VA does not have the same statutory obligation as the Department of Defense (DoD) to provide services to the families of the severely disabled, it has still provided benefits and services for more than 326,000 spouses, children, and parents of deceased service members who died on active duty or of service-connected conditions at the end of FY 2006. These survivors were receiving more than $4.3 billion in annual service-connected death benefits at that time.[7]

The majority of today's veterans served during times of war. Out of the total veteran population of over 24 million, over 70 percent (over 17 million) served during times when this nation was engaged in major conflicts. This includes 2.3 million living veterans who served in World War II, 2.3 million who served during the Korean War, over 7 million from Vietnam, nearly 5 million who served during the time of the first Gulf War, and nearly 970,000 veterans who served since 9/11 in the wars in Iraq and Afghanistan.

According to the VA, some 13 million, or over half the total number of veterans today, are over the age of 60, over 9 million are over the age of 65, and nearly 3 million are over the age of 80.

World War II and Korea Veterans

There are more than 4.6 million World War II and Korea-era veterans still alive (see Table 4.1). Together these veterans represent nearly 20 percent of the entire veteran population, a majority of whom are 20 years passed retirement age. As these veterans continue to die in large numbers, the overall current veteran population is beginning to decline. Consequently, the veteran population is projected to shrink by nearly 37 percent by 2030 because the large death rate is projected to exceed the rate of incoming veterans.[8]

Vietnam Veterans

There are over 7.1 million living Vietnam veterans, the majority of whom are between the ages of 55 and 69. The VA estimates that the majority of veterans from the Vietnam era will be 65 or older by 2011. As this large

Table 4.1 Current Veteran Demographics by Age and Period of Wartime Service

Age	All Veterans	Peacetime Veterans	War Time Veterans	Gulf War Only	Vietnam Only	Korean Conflict Only	WW II Only
<20	9,726	0	9,726	9,726	0	0	0
20–24	295,651	0	295,651	295,651	0	0	0
25–29	758,913	0	758,913	758,913	0	0	0
30–34	862,843	2,931	859,912	859,912	0	0	0
35–39	1,185,363	113,520	1,071,843	1,071,843	0	0	0
40–44	1,523,588	708,977	814,611	814,611	0	0	0
45–49	1,875,071	1,275,388	599,683	589,941	9,094	0	0
50–54	1,941,693	986,349	955,344	330,963	559,206	0	0
55–59	2,378,852	228,654	2,150,198	109,977	1,890,225	0	0
60–64	3,369,477	147,437	3,222,040	32,084	3,091,367	0	0
65–69	2,270,757	959,132	1,311,625	3,170	1,276,821	0	0
70–74	2,018,123	1,234,280	783,843	1,152	249,715	457,932	0
75–79	2,039,109	257,802	1,781,307	147	37,257	1,546,705	46,705
80–84	1,623,523	48,927	1,574,596	0	8,217	289,078	1,102,136
85–89	971,216	13,100	958,116	0	2,833	10,322	870,813
90+	318,582	10,076	308,507	0	405	2,695	286,255
Grand Total	**23,442,489**	**5,986,574**	**17,455,916**	**4,878,090**	**7,125,139**	**2,306,732**	**2,305,909**

Note: This table does not include the approximately 970,000 veterans from OEF/OIF.
Source: Department of Veterans Affairs, August 14, 2008.

segment of the veteran population ages, they too will be seeking benefits from the VA system in large numbers, filing new and reopened claims. According to the VA, as this segment of the population ages, "the demand for geriatric and all forms of long-term care should increase significantly relative to acute care. In particular, nursing home care policies, programs, and services will require continual monitoring and assessment."[9]

Consequently, while the overall veteran population is decreasing, the rate at which the new wave of aging veterans (mostly Vietnam-era veterans) use VA benefits is increasing, and this trend is expected to continue.[10] Consequently, the reduced burden placed on the VA by the steady passing of World War II and Korea-era veterans will be offset by the steady aging of Vietnam-era veterans who now represent the largest segment of the veteran population.

Many Vietnam veterans continue to suffer from a number of physical and psychological injuries incurred during their service in Southeast Asia. As noted in Chapter 2, most prevalent among these injuries is Posttraumatic Stress Disorder (PTSD). A National Vietnam Veterans Readjustment study conducted by the VA reported that nearly 31 percent of male Vietnam veterans and 27 percent of female veterans have reported suffering from PTSD during their lifetimes.[11] Those with high levels of war-zone exposure had significantly higher rates, with nearly 36 percent of men with high war-zone exposure meeting criteria for PTSD.

As a result of conditions related to PTSD, the readjustment study found that Vietnam veterans were more likely than their civilian counterparts to develop alcohol dependence, anxiety disorders, and antisocial behavior issues.[12] Additionally, many Vietnam veterans suffered and continue to suffer from readjustment issues such as marital and family problems and occupational instability.[13] Those with PTSD also reported greater incidence of physical health problems than other veterans or civilians.[14]

Additionally, a medical study conducted by the Sisters of Charity of Nazareth Health System found that Vietnam veterans suffering from PTSD were between 50 percent to 150 percent more likely than non-PTSD suffering veterans to suffer from other irregularities such as "circulatory, digestive, musculoskeletal, respiratory, infectious, and other serious diseases" even 20 years after seeing combat.[15] Moreover, some female Vietnam veterans have suffered from health problems that have led to severe birth defects among their children.[16]

The Veterans Health Administration has recently witnessed a dramatic increase in the use of VA mental health services among Vietnam-era veterans diagnosed with PTSD. The increase has been five times greater than that observed among Gulf-era veterans.[17] "But, while the patient load has been increasing, the number of clinic visits per veteran is decreasing, dropping by about 38 percent from 1997 to 2005. Fewer visits may mean poorer continuity of care and increased risk of veterans' prematurely dropping out of treatment."[18]

Gulf War Veterans

Veterans from the 1990–1991 Persian Gulf War are much younger than their counterparts from Vietnam; the majority of them are under the age of 44.[19] They are considered to be in the prime of life and are generally the age demographic that should be least in need of specialized care from the VA. The astonishingly low casualty rate—458 Americans were wounded in action during the first Gulf War—means that the VA has not had to provide care for large numbers of severely wounded troops.

Yet, the low number of combat-related injuries incurred by service members during the first Persian Gulf War belies the disproportionately large number of Gulf War veterans who suffer from other serious disorders related to their service in the Gulf. Most of these claims are for Gulf War Syndrome (GWS), a diverse set of disorders of the central nervous system stemming from service members' time in the Gulf when they were exposed to toxic chemicals including pesticides and drugs administered to protect troops against nerve gas. Soldiers experiencing GWS suffer from symptoms including dizziness, headaches, muscle pain or fatigue, diarrhea, and chest pain.[20] Several government studies have attempted to discredit Gulf War Syndrome, stating that it is merely a manifestation of the stress of war. However, research has shown that many Gulf War veterans have undergone significant neurological changes resulting in a host of medical issues. It has been suggested that these neurological changes leave Gulf War vets twice as likely to develop the fatal brain condition ALS, also known as Lou Gehrig's disease.

According to the VA's statistics—while only 458 military personnel were wounded in action—to date, a staggering 280,000 Gulf War veterans—or nearly half of those deployed to the combat zone—have filed claims with the VA for care and benefits, of which 212,000 or about 76 percent have been approved, over 30,000 have been denied, and nearly 39,000 are still pending.[21] This is an amazingly high number of noncombat-related injuries compared to combat-related injuries; but the claimants are and will be entitled to VA health care and disability benefits for many decades to come. As will be discussed in the following section, like Gulf War veterans, the ratio of combat-related injuries in Iraq and Afghanistan to the number of veterans seeking VA care and benefits is markedly disproportionate.

An extensive federal report released in December 2008 concluded that roughly one in four of the 697,000 U.S. veterans of the 1990–1991 Gulf War suffer from Gulf War illness. The over 400-page report concluded that "scientific evidence leaves no question that Gulf War illness is a real condition with real causes and serious consequences for affected veterans." The report "brings to a close one of the darkest chapters in the legacy of the 1991 Gulf War," said Anthony Hardie, a member of the congressionally mandated Research Advisory Committee on Gulf War Veterans' Illness and a member of the advocacy group Veterans of Modern Warfare. "This is a bittersweet victory, [because] this is what Gulf War veterans have been saying all along," Hardie said. "Years were squandered by the federal government . . . trying to disprove that anything could be wrong with Gulf War veterans."[22]

Global War on Terror Veterans

According to data obtained through the Freedom of Information Act from the Department of Defense and provided for this study by Veterans for Common Sense, a Washington-based nonprofit veterans advocacy group, as of the end of 2008 slightly more than 1.8 million U.S. troops have served in Operation Enduring Freedom in Afghanistan and Operation Iraqi Freedom. Of those, about 970,000, or slightly more than 50 percent, have left the military, while another 860,000 still remain. Once discharged from the military, veterans are eligible for free VA health care for five years and, depending on their injuries, will be entitled to veterans benefits and health care for the rest of their lives.

Given the bipartisan commitment to waging the war in Afghanistan until U.S. objectives are met and the fact that, under the U.S.-Iraqi Status of Forces Agreement (SOFA), the majority of U.S. forces will not leave Iraq until the end of 2011, large numbers of American troops will continue to be needed in both theaters in the years to come. Accordingly, hundreds of thousands of new recruits on top of the 860,000 servicemen and women still in Iraq and Afghanistan will, upon leaving the military, continue to place a heavy strain on the VA system.

Increased Racial, Ethnic, and Sexual Diversity in the Services

The ratio of women to men among the veteran population will increase in the coming decades. As the overall number of older (predominantly male) veterans decreases in the coming years, "women will account for more than 10 percent of the veteran population in 2020, up from 7 percent in 2006. DoD projects that the percentage of women will continue to increase—especially African-American women, which will rise at greater rate than that of African-American men."

As ethnic diversity continues to increase among Americans, the Veterans Benefit Commission found that by 2050 the population of veterans will reflect these ethnographic shifts. The Caucasian portion of the veteran population is expected to drop by 20 percent by 2050, as non-Caucasian populations will increase: black (from 8% to 12%), Hispanic (from 2% to 16%), and Asian (from 2% to 7%).[23]

As racial, ethnic, and sexual diversity among veterans increases, the VA will face new challenges providing equal health care to women and minority patients. According to a recent VHA report to the House Appropriations Committee, outpatient quality scores for women were lower than those for men in many facilities and African American veterans were less satisfied with their health care than were white veterans. While the VHA could not determine if deficiencies in patients' perceptions of their health care correlated with differences in quality of care, the results were nonetheless troublesome.[24] Given the projected increase in racial, sexual and ethnic diversity among veterans, these disparities will have to be addressed.

The current veteran population's shrinking numbers mask the fact that today's veterans are increasingly seeking more specialized, long-term care from the VA. As noted above, today's current veterans will continue to place stress on the VA system for years to come. But in order to understand the real demand that will be placed upon the VA in the near future, it is necessary to understand several aspects of the wars in Iraq and Afghanistan that will have profound implications for the future of veteran care.

Projecting the Future of Veteran Care: Unique Aspects of the Wars in Iraq and Afghanistan

Five aspects of the ongoing wars in Iraq and Afghanistan ensure that the veteran care system will be providing for a large number of veterans with an array of severe and complicated physical and mental injuries for many decades to come. The data and analysis below provide a sense of the scale and severity of physical and psychological injuries incurred by today's service members. Together, these factors pose new challenges to which the massive bureaucracies of the Department of Defense and Department of Veterans Affairs have been slow to respond.

1) The actual number of soldiers physically injured in Iraq and Afghanistan is far higher than the number commonly reported by DoD.

According to data provided by the DoD, as of February 2009, about 34,000 soldiers had been wounded in Iraq and Afghanistan. However, the figure provided by the DoD at that time included only soldiers injured while performing what the DoD considers "combat-related duties," while it excluded soldiers injured while performing "noncombat related duties." This latter category includes injuries incurred in accidents while on base, car accidents while on patrol, other accidents while in the theater, and soldiers medically evacuated for injuries or illnesses not directly related to combat.

In order to prevent the American public from becoming aware of the real costs of the wars in Iraq and Afghanistan, particularly the former, the Department of Defense continues to maintain two sets of books, one set of books for those who are wounded in combat, and another for those who are wounded in other ways. Upon examining the DoD's classification methods for noncombat-related related injuries, one finds that their metrics are somewhat arbitrary. For example, if a soldier or marine is traveling in either Iraq or Afghanistan by vehicle or helicopter at night (typically because traveling during the daytime in certain areas of either country during the day is highly dangerous) and his or her vehicle crashes, this is counted as a noncombat-related injury. Similarly, if a soldier or marine is traveling in a long convoy and the vehicle at the front of the convoy is struck by an Improvised Explosive Device (IED) and a vehicle at the back of the convoy crashes with the lead vehicles, those injured in the back of the convoy would not be counted as a combat-related injury while only those injured at the front of the convoy would.[25]

As indicated in Table 4.2, if one adds soldiers with noncombat-related injuries to the number of soldiers wounded in direct combat, the number of casualties as of February 2009 nearly triples to over 80,000.

While the actual number of soldiers injured in Iraq and Afghanistan is much higher than the number officially acknowledged by the Department

Table 4.2 Department of Defense Battlefield Casualties from OEF/OIF

Casualty Category	Iraq War	Afghanistan War	Both Wars
Deaths	4,228	640	4,868
Wounded in Action	31,010	2,686	33,696
Medically Evacuated Due to Injury or Disease	35,841	7,581	43,422
Total Casualties	**71,079**	**10,907**	**81,986**

Source: Veterans for Common Sense. Data Last Updated February 9, 2009.

of Defense, the overall number of Iraq and Afghanistan veterans seeking VA care is much higher still. As was the case in the first Gulf War, the ratio of noncombat-related injuries in Iraq and Afghanistan to the number of veterans seeking VA care and benefits is markedly disproportionate. As of January 2009, over 400,000 Operation Enduring Freedom/Operation Iraqi Freedom (OEF/OIF) veterans have filed for VA care. These claims encompass all eight of the VA's priority groups and include veterans with all types of physical and mental injuries (see Table 4.3).[26]

As the number of OEF/OIF veterans still in the service return home in the coming years, the number of veterans who seek VA care and benefits will increase considerably. According to a groundbreaking study by Dr. Linda Bilmes, Professor of Public Policy at Harvard's Kennedy School, based on analysis of the data from veterans of the first Gulf War, a total of approximately 800,000 veterans of the Iraq/Afghan wars will eventually seek VA care and disability benefits.[27]

Together these figures represent a much larger number than the misleading 34,000 figure acknowledged by the Pentagon, and must be taken into consideration while considering the future of veterans affairs. Given the current lengthy and repeated deployments, however, many veterans organizations have suggested that even Bilmes' estimates are too conservative. Indeed, it may well be that the number of eventual claims will rise to one million.

2) Second, today's prolonged and repeated deployment cycles significantly increase the risk of psychological injuries.

The extended nature of the conflicts in Afghanistan and Iraq has subjected the U.S. military to demands that it was not sized, resourced, or configured to meet at the time.[28] Today's all-volunteer force, particularly the Army component, as General John Abizaid, the CENTCOM Commander from 2003 to 2007, noted in the fall of 2006, was not "built to

Table 4.3 Number of Veterans Health Administration Patients from OEF/OIF

Category	Number of Veterans	Percent
Veteran Patients	400,304	41% of Veterans
Mental Health Patients	178,483	45% of Patients
PTSD Patients	105,465	26% of Patients
Vet Center Patients	302,503	31% of Veterans

Source: Veterans for Common Sense. Data Last Updated January 15, 2009.

sustain a long war." Because the Bush administration refused to face up to the manpower implications of its open-ended commitment of forces—particularly in Iraq—by reinstituting the draft, it has been forced to take three disastrous steps.

First, active duty forces have been deployed and redeployed without sufficient "dwell time." The Army's brigade combat teams have spent an average of 30 months in combat areas since 2002. Of the Army's 44 combat brigades, all but the First Brigade of the Second Infantry Division, which is permanently based in South Korea, have served at least one tour. Of the brigades that have served more than one tour:

- Sixteen brigades have had two tours in Iraq or Afghanistan.
- Fifteen brigades have had three tours in Iraq or Afghanistan.
- Five brigades have had four tours in Iraq or Afghanistan.[29]

Second, the task of sustaining troop levels in large numbers in Iraq and Afghanistan has forced the Army to violate its own deployment policy frequently. Army policy holds that after 12 months of deployment in a combat zone, troops should receive 24 months at home for "dwell time"—time at home between deployments to rest, recuperate, reconnect with family, integrate new unit members, train, and prepare to deploy again—before returning to combat. Even before President Bush sent an additional 30,000 troops to Iraq in 2007, the Army was forced to break its own dwell time policy and initiated a 12 month deployed to 12 month dwell time ratio. Once the surge began, the Pentagon was forced once again to break its policy and extended Army deployments to 15 months with 12 months of dwell time. Similarly, Marine units have had seven month deployment cycles for every six months at home. While deployment times for Army units returned to 12 months (with 12 months between deployments) in the fall of 2008, many Army units on their second or third tour were made to endure harsh 15 month deployments, tours that are expected to have a significant impact on soldiers' mental and physical health in the future.

Third, National Guard and reserve units have been transformed from a strategic to an operational reserve. As with active units, the Pentagon has been forced to break its own National Guard deployment policy, which requires soldiers from the reserve component to have a five to one deployment to dwell time ratio, in order to keep large numbers of soldiers deployed to Iraq and Afghanistan. Today, many Army Guard soldiers are on a one year deployed to one year dwell time ratio.[30]

According to several highly publicized studies, the length and frequency of deployments to combat zones directly increases the incidence of psychological injuries. Additionally, recent Army studies have revealed that soldiers serving repeated deployments are 50 percent more likely than those serving one tour to experience acute combat stress, which significantly raises their risk of suffering Posttraumatic Stress Disorder (PTSD).[31]

These studies' findings are confirmed by a report issued in early 2008 by the Office of the Surgeon General for the United States Army Medical Command (MHAT V). MHAT V conclusively found that frequency and length of deployments significantly increase a service member's risk of developing psychological problems.

> *Multiple Deployments.* According to the Surgeon General's report: "Soldiers on their third or fourth deployment were at significantly higher risk than Soldiers on their first or second deployment [to experience] mental health problems and work-related problems. A Non-Commissioned Officer (NCO) on his or her second or third/fourth deployment reports significantly more mental health problems (adjusted percent of 27.2%) than does an NCO on his or her second deployment (adjusted percent of 18.5%) and significantly more than an NCO on his or her first deployment (adjusted percent of 11.9%)."[32]

> *Deployment Length.* The Surgeon General also notes that, "Reports of work-related problems due to stress, mental health problems and marital separations generally increased with each subsequent month of the deployment. Behavioral health results suggest that the post six-month period is a heightened risk time for mental health problems and that reports of mental health problems level off in the months immediately before redeployment (possibly due to anticipation of returning home). Nonetheless, the adjusted percent of Soldiers reporting mental health problems at month 15 is significantly higher than the percent reporting problems in the early months, and redeployment research strongly suggests that rates will rise when [the soldiers] return."[33]

Because the draft still existed during the war in Vietnam, the Department of Defense had a large pool of recruits upon which it could draw to send to the combat zone. Because the military had so many recruits to call on, very few soldiers or marines endured multiple deployments—a fact that led many experts to argue that America had fought a one-year war in Vietnam 10 times. As noted above, nearly 31 percent of male Vietnam veterans and 27 percent of female veterans reported suffering from PTSD during their lifetimes. In today's all-volunteer force, many soldiers and marines are forced to serve three or even four tours in combat. This facet of the current wars in Iraq and Afghanistan will ensure that psychological injuries will be far more widespread and severe than in previous conflicts. In fact, large numbers of psychological injuries are already beginning to be identified in today's returning veterans.

3) Lengthy and repeated deployments in Iraq and Afghanistan have inflicted a large number of service members with psychological and cognitive injuries.

While injuries such as Posttraumatic Stress Disorder (PTSD) and clinical depression are not unique to the wars in Iraq and Afghanistan, the number of veterans from Iraq and Afghanistan being diagnosed with and requesting long-term treatment for these types of psychological injuries is unprecedented. To date, approximately 18 percent of the over 1.8 million U.S. service members who have returned from Afghanistan and Iraq currently have Posttraumatic Stress Disorder or depression. According to a Department of Defense–sponsored study by the RAND Corporation, as many as 300,000 returning troops are potentially suffering from PTSD or major depression.[34]

While not all vets with psychological wounds file claims for their injuries, the number of claims beginning to be filed by military people diagnosed with such wounds is large and growing. According to the VA, from 1999 to 2007, the number of veterans receiving compensation benefits for PTSD increased from 120,000 to nearly 300,000.[35] According to the Department of Veterans Affairs' own predictions for PTSD disability claims, the number of claims that will be filed in the future will be staggering. In 2002, the VA projected about 335,000 claims. It now predicts that number will jump to 950,000 in 2008.[36]

Traumatic brain injuries (TBI) have also been incurred by a large number of soldiers and marines in both Iraq and Afghanistan. Along with PTSD, TBI has become the signature injury of today's wars. Sophisticated improvised explosive devises (IEDs), explosively formed penetrators (EFPs), and other highly lethal explosives frequently used against our soldiers in both theaters have not only been the cause of enormous numbers of U.S. casualties, but have left many thousands of troops with nonvisible scars of war.

While nonvisible, these wounds are no less serious. According to the RAND study quoted above, approximately 320,000 troops report having incurred a traumatic brain injury while deployed. Of those reporting a probable TBI, 57 percent—or over 182,000—have not been evaluated by a physician for the potential injury.

4) Fourth, the types of psychological and head injuries suffered by soldiers and marines in Iraq and Afghanistan often take years to recognize.

In a recent Army study, only four to five percent of soldiers were referred to mental health care upon their first Post-Deployment Health

Assessment, but at the second assessment, conducted three to six months later, the figure jumped to 20.3 percent for active duty soldiers and a staggering 42.4 percent for reserve component soldiers.[37]

In the second assessment, symptoms for PTSD jumped 40 percent from 11.8 percent to 16.7 percent; clinical depression more than doubled from 4.7 percent to 10.3 percent; issues relating to interpersonal conflict experienced a four-fold increase from 3.5 percent to 14.0 percent; and overall mental health issues increased by 60 percent from 17.0 percent to 27.1 percent.[38]

The fact that PTSD symptoms often take a considerable period of time after a traumatic experience to develop indicates that this will be a long-term problem facing the VA. Given the complexity and severity of the PTSD and TBI problem, these subjects will be discussed in greater detail in Chapter 6.

5) Finally, high numbers of soldiers are surviving battlefield injuries that would have been fatal in past conflicts.

Due to the extraordinary advances in battlefield medicine, protective equipment and medical transportation in recent years, far more soldiers are surviving serious injuries incurred in Iraq and Afghanistan than would have been the case in previous conflicts. According to the President's Commission on Care for America's Returning Wounded Warriors, also known as the Dole-Shalala Commission, "In the Vietnam era, five out of every eight seriously injured service members survived [their battlefield injuries]; today, seven out of eight survive, many with injuries that in previous wars would have been fatal."[39] Bilmes notes slightly different numbers in the study noted above:

> The ratio of wounded in combat to killed in Iraq is 7 to 1; in Vietnam, it was 2.6 to 1, and in World War II, 2 to 1. If all injuries are included, such as those from road accidents or debilitating illnesses, *Iraq has produced 15 wounded for every single fatality.*[40]

Today's high survival rates are in large part due to extraordinary advances in battlefield medicine. Indeed, throughout our history, some of the greatest advances in medicine have come about in times of war and the tradition continues today. According to a recent *USA Today* analysis of military medicine, the Pentagon is taking advantage of new lifesaving equipment for use on the battlefields in Iraq and Afghanistan, including dehydrated blood products that can be stored up to two years, a portable battlefield device that stops internal bleeding with ultrasound, and a nonaddictive painkiller as powerful as morphine. Additionally, battlefield doctors are able take advantage of tools not yet approved for use in the United States such as a portable heart-lung machine developed in Germany that helps wounded soldiers breathe.[41]

Advances in long-distance air evacuation have also played a large role in the number of severely injured soldiers surviving battlefield wounds. In order to rush critically wounded soldiers to theater, regional, and eventually American hospitals, the military has created a fleet of "flying hospitals;" C-130s and other military cargo plains retrofitted with advanced medical equipment and staffed with surgeons, doctors and nurses to treat patients while en route to hospitals.

> The Air Force's system of using specially configured aircraft to move thousands of casualties from war zones almost daily didn't exist during Vietnam, the last war in which large numbers of casualties were routinely evacuated to the USA. In those days, doctors typically waited up to *six weeks* for patients to become stable enough to complete the trip home, said Dale Smith, a professor of medical history at the Uniformed Services University of the Health Sciences in Bethesda, Md.
>
> Now, because of new treatment methods and technology on the aircraft, the most critically injured patients can make the trip *in a few days*. "They've really thought about this very carefully, no wasted moments, no wasted movements," Rather than try to re-create in Iraq or Afghanistan sophisticated hospitals such as Landstuhl, the military has built smaller field hospitals where patients are treated and stabilized. Doctors in Iraq now leave many wounds open and vacuum-sealed with plastic. That also was not possible in Vietnam. "Now the sickest of sick patients can get on that airplane," said Air Force Maj. Timothy Woods, a general surgeon at Landstuhl.[42]

This higher survival rate is welcome news. But it has also significantly increased the demand on the VA in the areas of critical care, outpatient care, and rehabilitation. It has also increased the number and complexity of injuries suffered by the military personnel surviving their wounds to include service members with multiple trauma, visible, and nonvisible injuries.

It is important to note that these survival rates will leave the United States with a legacy of providing medical care and paying disability benefits to a large number of veterans and in some cases their dependents for many decades to come.[43]

The five points discussed above indicate that the scope and the severity of the medical problems—physical, psychological, and cognitive—facing today's returning veterans will be much larger than the VA has demonstrated it is capable of managing. Recognizing this, it is important to evaluate the administrative barriers that these service men and women face when attempting to access VA care.

Notes

1. Department of Veterans Affairs, "FY 07 VA Information Pamphlet," http://www1.va.gov/vetdata/docs/Pamphlet_2-1-08.pdf.

2. Congressional Research Service, "The Cost of Iraq, Afghanistan, and Other Global War on Terror Operations Since 9/11," Summary, http://www.fas.org/sgp/crs/natsec/RL33110.pdf.

3. Ibid.

4. Joesph Stiglitz and Linda Bilmes, *The Three Trillion Dollar War: The True Cost of the Iraq Conflict* (New York: W. W. Norton, 2008), 81–82.

5. Rick Maze, "McCain: Make Combat-Disabled Top VA Priority," *Army Times,* July 24, 2008. http://www.armytimes.com/news/2008/07/military_mccain_healthcare_072308/.

6. David Zucchino, "Injured Veterans Engaged in New Combat," *Los Angeles Times,* November 25, 2008.

7. Veterans Benefit Commission, "Chapter 3: Veterans' Past, Present and Future," 48, http://www.vetscommission.org/pdf/Veterans_Past_Present_Future-ch-3.pdf.

8. Ibid., 51.

9. Ibid., 51.

10. Ibid.

11. Jennifer L. Price, "Findings of the National Vietnam Veterans' Readjustment Study," U.S. Department of Veterans Affairs. http://www.ncptsd.va.gov/ncmain/ncdocs/fact_shts/fs_nvvrs.html?opm=1&rr=rr45&srt=d&echorr=true.

12. Ibid.

13. Ibid.

14. Ibid.

15. "Vietnam Combat Linked to Many Diseases 20 Years Later," *Science Daily,* November 26, 1997. http://www.sciencedaily.com/releases/1997/11/971126042926.htm.

16. U.S. Department of Veterans Affairs, "Benefits for Women Vietnam Veterans' Children with Birth Defects," http://www.vba.va.gov/bln/21/topics/women/birth.htm.

17. RAND Corporation, "Invisible Wounds of War," 268, http://www.rand.org/pubs/monographs/2008/RAND_MG720.pdf.

18. Ibid.

19. Data provided by the Department of Veterans Affairs. Received upon request August 14, 2008.

20. Research Advisory Committee on Gulf War Veterans' Illnesses, http://www1.va.gov/rac-gwvi/docs/Minutes_Dec2005.pdf.

21. Department of Veterans Affairs, "Gulf War Veterans Information System," May 2007 (cf. Preface, note 8), 7, http://ngwrc.org/pdfs/GWVIS-2007-may.pdf.

22. Alan Silverleib, "Gulf War Illness is Real, New Federal Report Says," CNN, November 17, 2008. http://www.cnn.com/2008/HEALTH/11/17/gulf.war.illness. study/index.html.

23. Veterans Benefit Commission, "Chapter 3: Veterans' Past, Present and Future," 52.

24. Department of Veterans Affairs, "Report to the Appropriations Committee of the U.S. House of Representatives in response to House Appropriations Report No. 110–186, accompanying Public Law 110–161, The Consolidated Appropriations Act, 2008," P. 6–7, http://www1.va.gov/health/docs/Hospital_Quality_Report.pdf.

25. For more on the Department of Defense's classification methods, see "Financial Costs of the War in Iraq," Center for American Progress, March 27, 2008, http://www.americanprogress.org/events/2008/03/costiraq.html.

26. For more information of the VA's eight-tiered priority ranking system, please see: http://www.va.gov/healtheligibility/Library/pubs/HealthCareOverview/#Overview.

27. Testimony of Linda Bilmes before the House Committee on Veterans' Affairs, February 14, 2008, http://veterans.house.gov/hearings/Testimony. aspx?TID=33407&Newsid=189&Name=%20Linda%20J.%20Bilmes.

28. RAND Corporation, "Invisible Wounds of War," 23.

29. "Brigade Combat Team Deployments," *Army Times,* October 3, 2008.

30. Lawrence J. Korb and Sean Duggan, "Caught off Guard: The Link Between Our National Security and Our National Guard," May 2007, http://www. americanprogress.org/issues/2007/05/national_guard.html.

31. Ann Scott Tyson, "Repeat Iraq Tours Raise Risk of PTSD, Army Finds," *Washington Post,* December 20, 2006.

32. Army Surgeon General, United States Army Medical Command, "Mental Health Advisory Team V," 46, http://www.armymedicine.army.mil/reports/mhat/ mhat_v/MHAT_V_OIFandOEF-Redacted.pdf.

33. Ibid., 42.

34. RAND Corporation, "Invisible Wounds of War," 103.

35. Government Accountability Office, "Veterans' Disability Benefits: Claims Processing Challenges Persist, while VA Continues to Take Steps to Address Them," February 14, 2008, 6, http://www.gao.gov/new.items/d08473t.pdf.

36. Veterans for Common Sense, "Forgotten Soldiers," November 9, 2007, http://www.veteransforcommonsense.org/articleid/8748.

37. Elizabeth Lorge, "Army Study Finds Delayed Combat Stress Reporting," U.S. Army, November 14, 2007, http://www.army.mil/-news/2007/11/14/6090-army-study-finds-delayed-combat-stress-reporting/.

38. Charles Milliken, Jennifer Auchterlonie, and Charles Hoge, "Longitudinal Assessment of Mental Health Problems Among Active and Reserve Component Soldiers Returning from the Iraq War," *The Journal of the American Medical Association* 298, no. 18 (2007): 2141–2148, http://jama.ama-assn.org/cgi/content/

abstract/298/18/2141?maxtoshow=&HITS=10&hits=10&RESULTFORMAT=
&fulltext=post-deployment&searchid=1&FIRSTINDEX=0&resourcetype=HWCIT.

39. Report of the President's Commission on Care for America's Returning Wounded Warriors, http://www.veteransforamerica.org/wp-content/uploads/2008/12/presidents-commission-on-care-for-americas-returning-wounded-warriors-report-july-2007.pdf, 2.

40. Linda Bilmes, "Iraq's 100 Year Mortgage," *Foreign Policy Magazine,* March/April 2008, http://www.foreignpolicy.com/users/login.php?story_id=4175&URL=http://www.foreignpolicy.com/story/cms.php?story_id=4175 (emphasis added).

41. Gregg Zoroya, "Lifesaving Knowledge, Innovation Emerge in War Clinic," *USA Today,* March 27, 2006, http://www.usatoday.com/news/world/iraq/2006-03-26-war-clinics_x.htm.

42. Ibid. (emphasis added).

43. Bilmes, "Iraq's 100 Year Mortgage."

CHAPTER 5

Administrative Barriers to Accessing VA Health Care and Benefits

Sean E. Duggan

Sure, it's not hard to find vets who complain about difficulties in establishing eligibility. Many are outraged that the Bush administration has decided to deny previously promised health-care benefits to veterans who don't have service-related illnesses or who can't meet a strict means test. Yet these grievances are about *access* to the system, not about the quality of care received by those who get in.

—Phillip Longman,
Best Care Anywhere (emphasis added)

The above quotation from Phillip Longman, health care expert and author of the acclaimed book on the VA health care system *Best Care Anywhere,* illustrates forcefully the fact that the greatest barriers veterans face in receiving quality health care from the VA comes more from difficulties accessing VA health care than from receiving poor care when they are finally in the system.

In fact, the majority of veterans who are able to access VA health care in a timely fashion receive excellent care. This is in large part due to the VA's integrated health care system, its patient care coordination, chronic disease management and emphasis on long-term preventive care.[1] The VA's health care mission "cover[s] the continuum of care providing inpatient and outpatient care; a wide range of services, such as pharmacy, prosthetics, and mental health; long-term care in both institutional and non-institutional settings; and other health care programs such as...readjustment counseling."[2]

The Veterans Health Administration (VHA) has the responsibility of providing care for a large number of patients with diverse and complicated needs. In order to meet these needs, the VA, through the VHA, operates one of the largest and most integrated health care systems in the nation. It consists of 153 hospitals, 882 ambulatory care and community-based outpatient clinics, 207 Vet Centers, 136 nursing homes, 45 residential rehabilitation treatment programs and 92 comprehensive home care programs.[3] Moreover, more than $37 billion or about half of the VA's total expenditures in fiscal year 2007 belonged to its health care and research budget ($37.3 billion in FY07).[4]

Despite its broad mandate and the unique and complicated needs of its patients, the VHA's quality indicators have actually increased in recent years. Recent studies by the *New England Journal of Medicine* comparing VA health facilities on 11 measures of quality with fee-for-service Medicare have shown that on all 11 measures, the quality of care in veterans facilities proved to be "significantly better." In another study conducted in 2005 by the National Committee for Quality Assurance, which ranks health care plans on 17 different performance measures, VHA facilities outperformed the highest rated non-VHA hospitals in every single category. As Phillip Longman points out, winning NCQA's seal of approval is the gold standard in the health care industry.[5]

Additionally, the VA's Clinical Practice Guidelines Index (which measures the degree to which a provider follows nationally recognized standards of care) and the VA's Prevention Index II (which tracks compliance with clinical guidelines for preventive care) have both improved since 2002.[6]

When compared to national external composite benchmarks developed by VHA, the agency's facilities excel in both outpatient and inpatient medical care. According to the Facility Health care Effectiveness Data and Information Set (or HEDIS, a tool used by more than 90 percent of America's health plans to measure performance on important dimensions of care and service) outpatient composite scores exceeded national outpatient composite scores at all VHA facilities.[7] Similarly Facility ORYX (a tool to measure performance of inpatient care service) inpatient composite scores exceeded the national external inpatient composite benchmark score at 123 of 124 VHA facilities.[8]

Moreover, according to the American Consumer Satisfaction Index, veterans themselves consistently rank their overall satisfaction with VA health care higher than patients rank Medicare and Medicaid. In a recent survey, 81 percent of VHA hospital patients expressed satisfaction with the care they received, compared to 77 percent of Medicare and Medicaid patients.[9]

Given these laudable quality indicators, the quality of care that veterans receive once in the VA health care system will not be the main focus of this chapter. This is not to say that the VA health care system does not have its fair share of problems. However, an analysis of the impediments veterans face in accessing that care is a more critical area and therefore will be the topic of this chapter.

Many of these impediments are the inevitable consequence of the sheer number of veterans seeking care discussed in Chapter 4. Put simply, today's volume exceeds the VA's capacity to provide for such a large number of veterans with diverse and complicated needs, as "the demand for VA medical treatment far outstrips supply."[10] Consequently, the VA has been forced to rely on its priority ranking system and waiting lists to control the number of veterans it can treat. Other impediments are the result of administrative hurdles inherent in the complicated process veterans must navigate in order to receive VA care.

Together, the increasingly large number of veterans demanding care and benefits from the VA and administrative redundancies and inefficiencies built into the process of receiving VA care have greatly reduced the ability of veterans to access that care.

Increased Demand on the VA

The VA health care system underwent sweeping restructuring beginning in 1994 that dramatically expanded the number of veterans entitled to VA health care and benefits. Reforms put into place beginning at that time culminated in the passage of the Veterans Health care Eligibility Reform Act of 1996. "Before the law was passed, the only individuals allowed free access to the VA health care system were those deemed disabled or indigent by VA standards or belonging to a special group (e.g., former prisoners of war). After the law's implementation, the VA implemented a means test...[which] placed each veteran in one of seven [there are currently eight] priority groups based on an array of factors including level of disability, level of income, and POW status." The law's passage "also enabled [the] VA to eliminate the distinction between hospitalization and outpatient care and to provide prevention services and primary care."

As a consequence of the restructuring, the number of veterans entitled to VA health care and benefits increased substantially. "The number of unique patients treated in the VA health care system rose from 3.0 million in FY 1998 (before enrollment) to 3.4 million in FY 2000 (one year after enrollment began) to 4.9 million in FY 2006."[11] In Fiscal Year 2007 alone, the VHA provided care for over 5.5 million unique patients.[12] This means that in 2007, VHA provided health care services to over 80 percent more patients than it did in 1998. Moreover, VHA staff is treating more out-patients than ever before, recently increasing by nearly five percent a year (the VA handled 53.4 million outpatient visits in 2006 and 55.7 million in 2007).[13]

VETERAN HEALTH CARE

Who Is Eligible?

A person who served in the active military, naval, or air service and who was discharged or released under conditions other than dishonorable may qualify for VA health care benefits. Reservists and National Guard members may also qualify for VA health care benefits if they were called to active duty. Once enrolled, veterans can receive health care at VA health care facilities anywhere in the country.

Minimum Duty Requirements

Veterans who enlisted after Sept. 7, 1980, or who entered active duty after Oct. 16, 1981, must have served 24 continuous months or the full period for they were called to active duty in order to be eligible. This minimum duty requirement may not apply to veterans discharged for hardship, early out or a disability incurred or aggravated in the line of duty.

Priority Groups

During enrollment, each veteran is assigned to a priority group. The VA uses priority groups to balance demand for VA health care enrollment (available) with resources. Changes in available resources may reduce the number of priority groups The VA can enroll. If this occurs, The VA will publicize the changes and notify affected enrollees. A description of priority groups follows:

> **Group 1:** Veterans with service-connected disabilities rated 50 percent or more and/or veterans determined by the VA to be unemployable due to service-connected conditions.
>
> **Group 2:** Veterans with service-connected disabilities rated 30 or 40 percent.
>
> **Group 3:** Veterans with service-connected disabilities rated 10 and 20 percent, veterans who are former Prisoners of War (POW) or were awarded a Purple Heart medal, veterans awarded special eligibility for disabilities incurred in treatment or participation in a VA Vocational Rehabilitation program, and

veterans whose discharge was for a disability incurred or aggravated in the line of duty.

Group 4: Veterans receiving aid and attendance or housebound benefits and/ or veterans determined by the VA to be catastrophically disabled.

Group 5: Veterans receiving VA pension benefits or eligible for Medicaid programs, and nonservice-connected veterans and noncompensable, zero percent service-connected veterans whose gross annual household income and net worth are below the established VA means test thresholds.

Group 6: Veterans of World War I; veterans seeking care solely for certain conditions associated with exposure to radiation; for any illness associated with combat service in a war after the Gulf War or during a period of hostility after Nov. 11, 1998; for any illness associated with participation in tests conducted by the Department of Defense (DoD) as part of Project 112/Project SHAD; and veterans with zero percent service-connected disabilities who are receiving disability compensation benefits.

Group 7: Nonservice-connected veterans and non-compensable, zero-percent service-connected veterans with household income and/or net worth above the VA's national income threshold, but whose household income is below the geographically-based income threshold for their resident location.

Group 8: All other nonservice-connected veterans and zero percent, noncompensable service-connected veterans who agree to pay copays. (Note: Effective Jan. 17, 2003, the VA no longer enrolls new veterans into priority group 8).

Combat Veterans: Effective Jan. 28, 2008, veterans discharged from active duty on or after Jan. 28, 2003, are eligible for enhanced enrollment placement into Priority Group 6 (unless eligible for higher enrollment Priority Group placement) for 5 years post discharge. Veterans with combat service after Nov. 11, 1998, who were discharged from active duty before Jan. 28, 2003, and who apply for enrollment on or after Jan. 28, 2008, are eligible for this enhanced enrollment benefit through Jan. 27, 2011. Veterans, including activated reservists and members of the National Guard, are eligible if they served on active duty in a theater of combat operations after Nov. 11, 1998, and, have been discharged under other than dishonorable conditions.

Given the VA's large but finite resources, this increased demand has forced the agency to regulate the number of patients able to access VA care by implementing its priority ranking system and relying on waiting lists. Not surprisingly, these measures have prevented many veterans from receiving timely, high quality VA health care available to those patients who are already in the system. These bottlenecks are significant impediments to certain categories of veterans seeking the VA health care they deserve.

According to the Stiglitz/Bilmes study, "As the demand for medical care increases, the already overwhelmed Department of Veterans Affairs may be unable to meet it ... The quality of medical care is likely to continue to be high for those veterans treated in the new polytrauma centers, but the current state of service means that not all facilities can offer *such high quality in a timely fashion.*"[14]

Priority Rankings

According to the VA, "the number of veterans who can be enrolled in the [VA] health care program is determined by the amount of money Congress gives VA each year. Since funds are limited, VA set up priority groups to make sure that certain groups of veterans are able to be enrolled before others."[15] To ensure that the most seriously injured veterans receive proper care, the VA has used its priority ranking system to bump less-severely injured patients and those veterans with independent financial means from receiving VA medical care. Effective January 17, 2003, the VA stopped enrolling new veterans into priority group 8. As noted above, this has prevented some 400,000 veterans from receiving free VA health care since 2003.

Despite the group 8 restriction, large numbers of veterans are facing long waiting lists—especially in certain specialties—and in some cases simply an absence of care. As noted in Chapter 4, this is in large part due to the parallel increase in Vietnam veterans and Iraq and Afghanistan veterans seeking care. This dual surge has, according to a RAND corporation study, resulted in "competing service eras" that contend for the VA's limited resources.[16]

While in theory all veterans of the wars in Iraq and Afghanistan, including inactivated reservists, are eligible to receive health care services from the VA, the department's fixed budget and eight-tiered priority system have prevented certain groups of veterans from receiving timely VA care. According to Stiglitz and Bilmes, "not only do the increased needs of new veterans mean that sometimes they do not get the care they need; often they get served only by crowding out older veterans, who must wait longer—or may never get the care they need."[17]

Unfortunately, this crowding out goes both ways. As the recent RAND study notes, "VA has documented a surprisingly large increase in the number of Vietnam-era veterans using mental health services, greatly exceeding the increase in the number of OEF/OIF veterans. Increased demand for services from older veterans likely reflects recurrence of mental health problems and legitimate need. However, this dynamic may result in lowered access for lower-priority OEF/OIF veterans."[18]

It is important to note that the number of OEF/OIF veterans who will seek VA health care and benefits is certain to grow significantly in the coming years. According to the VA, "As in other cohorts of military veterans, the percentage of [Iraq and Afghanistan] veterans receiving medical care from the VA and the percentage of veterans with any type of diagnosis will tend to increase over time as these veterans continue to enroll for VA health care and to develop new health problems."[19] As of January 2009, approximately 400,000 of the 970,000 service members from Iraq and Afghanistan who have been discharged from military service and have entered or are entering the VA have so far sought treatment at VA facilities.[20]

This number is sure to grow, given the unique aspects of the wars in Iraq and Afghanistan outlined in Chapter 4. As the OEF/OIF veteran population continues to grow and seek care in large numbers, the VA will continue to face a series of tough choices on how to regulate the amount of patients it cares for.

Waiting Lists

VHA policy requires that all veterans with service-connected disability ratings of 50 percent or greater and all other veterans requiring care for service-connected disabilities be scheduled for care within 30 days of requested appointment dates. All other veterans must be scheduled for care within 120 days. VHA policy also requires that requests for appointments be acted on by the medical facility as soon as possible, but no later than 7 calendar days from the date of request.[21] Recent evidence shows that, faced with the dual surge in service members seeking care, the VA is currently unable to meet its own standards. According to a report released by the VA Office of the Inspector General (VAOIG), gaps in delivering timely patient care are beginning to show.

In a recent survey of 700 veterans who were meant to be seen by VHA within 30 days, the office of the Inspector General (VAOIG) found that only 524 (75%) of the 700 had been seen within 30 days of the desired date. As a result, 176 (25%) of the appointments VAOIG reviewed had waiting times over 30 days when VOIG used the desired date of care that was established and documented by the medical providers in the medical records.[22]

Upon reviewing the 176 cases where veterans' waiting times were more than 30 days, VAOIG identified 64 veterans that were given an appointment past the 30- or 120-day requirement and should have been on the electronic waiting lists. This represents 9 percent of the 700 appointments reviewed. Most troubling was that of the 64 cases, *36 were veterans with service-connected ratings of 50 percent or greater,* 12 were being treated for service-connected conditions, and 16 had waiting times more than 120 days.[23]

Also troubling, VAOIG found that the VHA's method of calculating the waiting times of new patients understated the actual waiting times. "Because of past problems associated with schedulers not entering the correct desired date when creating appointments, VHA uses the appointment creation date as the starting point for measuring the waiting times for new appointments. VHA acknowledges that this method could understate the actual waiting times for new patients by the number of days schedulers take to create the appointment."[24] While the VHA disagreed with VAOIG's conclusions,[25] the Inspector General found that waiting times could actually be much longer than originally thought.

The VA's waiting list problems demonstrate clearly the VHA's inability to provide medical care to service members from every era in a timely fashion. These waiting times, especially for severely injured service members, are potentially dangerous to the health of the veterans. Unfortunately, administrative impediments and bureaucratic inefficiencies present many veterans with other barriers to obtaining VA medical care and benefits.

Administrative Impediments to VA Care and Benefits

While the VA's priority ranking system and waiting lists have prevented certain categories of veterans from receiving care, administrative impediments potentially affect all veterans. The Independent Review Group, an independent panel commissioned by Secretary of Defense Robert Gates in the wake of the scandal at the Department of Defense's Walter Reed Army Medical Center, summarized well the complex and difficult process that injured service members and their families must navigate during their transition from Department of Defense to VA care:

> From the time a service member is wounded on the battlefield there begins a complex process of actions, reactions, and transitions, starting and continuing through: the immediate medical response and evacuation; the transportation and gathering of the family; inpatient care; outpatient care; rehabilitation; Medical Evaluation Board; Physical Evaluation Board; return to duty or transition to additional evaluations; and into the care of the Department of Veterans Affairs.[26]

During this long and complicated process, a number of impediments can and frequently do prevent service members from receiving necessary VA health care. And, once in the system, veterans seeking care often face other barriers that result from claims backlogs, lengthy appeals' processes, and other bureaucratic inefficiencies.

In order to present a better understanding of the difficulties veterans face in accessing VA health care and benefits, this section will analyze the interrelationships between the agencies within the Department of Veterans Affairs; these include the Veterans Health Administration (VHA) and the Veterans Benefit Administration (VBA). In addition, we will also discuss the role the Department of Defense (DoD) plays in creating impediments for veterans to receive VA care during the transition of patient care from the DoD to the VA.

The most common impediments veterans face in accessing VA health care result from:

1. Redundant DoD and VA disability evaluations;
2. Outdated and adversarial disability evaluations and criteria;
3. Poor patient case management and continuity of care;
4. Inadequate Department of Defense and Department of Veterans Affairs information sharing; and
5. Claims backlogs

While by no means exhaustive, these five impediments have prevented veterans from receiving the high quality health care and benefits that the VA can and should provide in a timely manner.

Clearly, some of the problems discussed in this chapter are also applicable to the U.S. civilian health care delivery system as a whole. In this sense, many of the challenges faced by the VA health care system are not just a VA problem but a national problem inherent in the delivery of health care service generally. Yet, because of intense media scrutiny, health care for service members returning from the wars in Iraq and Afghanistan has become a source of continued public outrage over the past two years.

Health care for returning service men and women was most recently thrust into the public consciousness in the wake of the February 2007 Walter Reed scandal. To be sure, Walter Reed Army Medical Center is part of the Department of Defense's medical system—not that of the VA—but the problems uncovered there prompted broader questions about whether the federal government was fully prepared to meet the health care needs of service members returning from combat.

If there was one positive outcome of the of Walter Reed scandal it is the fact that it triggered several high ranking congressional and presidential commissions that have reached a broad consensus on the problems veterans face in accessing VA health care and benefits. The following discussion is based upon analysis and conclusions from the following commissions:

- *Veteran's Disability Benefits Commission:* Honoring the Call to Duty: Veterans' Disability Benefits in the 21st century
- *The Dole-Shalala Commission:* Report of the President's Commission on Care for America's Returning Wounded Warriors
- *The Independent Review Group:* Report on Rehabilitative Care and Administrative Process at Walter Reed Army Medical Center and National Naval Medical Center

Despite broad recognition of the major administrative impediments veterans face when seeking access to VA health care and benefits *and* the measures needed to alleviate the problems they create, implementation of widely accepted solutions has not taken place. The fact that the impediments to proper and timely care are widely recognized but have not been acted upon makes it clear that both the DoD medical system and the VA remain on a peacetime footing nearly a decade after 9/11. As the following section will demonstrate, neither agency has undertaken comprehensive reform nor have they been given the funding needed to care properly for today's veterans and the flood of veterans it will receive in the future.

Redundant DoD and VA Disability Evaluations

According to Linda Bilmes and Joseph Stigletz, the primary impediment veterans face to accessing VA care "is the awkward, duplicative system by which wounded servicemen and women transition from military to veterans' status."[27] The transition from the DoD to the VA can be confusing, difficult and frustrating, particularly for seriously injured and recovering service members and their families.

The major cause of the confusion results from the fact that service members must undertake two separate disability evaluation processes, one from the DoD and one from the VA, that have separate purposes. The description from the Government Accountability Office (GAO) of the two disability evaluation processes is worth quoting at length given its accurate portrayal of the complicated process injured service members must navigate in their transition from the DoD to the VA:

> Returning injured service members must potentially navigate two different disability evaluation systems that generally rely on the same criteria but for different purposes. DoD's system serves as a personnel management process by identifying service members who are no longer medically fit for duty. The military's process starts with identification of a

medical condition that could render the service member unfit for duty, a process that could take months to complete. The service member goes through a medical evaluation proceeding [MEB], where medical evidence is evaluated, and potentially unfit conditions are identified.

The member then goes through a physical evaluation board (PEB) process, where a determination of fitness or unfitness for duty is made and, if found unfit for duty, a combined percentage rating is assigned for all unfit conditions and the service member is discharged from duty. The injured service member then receives monthly disability retirement payments if he or she meets the minimum rating and years of duty thresholds or, if not, a lump-sum severance payment.

...VA will evaluate all claimed conditions [by a separate VA evaluation board], *whether they were evaluated by the military service or not ... Although a service member may file a VA claim while still in the military, he or she can only obtain disability compensation from VA as a veteran ...* If the veteran is found to have one or more service-connected disabilities with a combined rating of at least 10 percent, VA will pay monthly compensation. The veteran can claim additional benefits, for example, if a service-connected disability worsens.[28]

Although service members can apply for VA benefits while still in the military, they must first obtain veteran status in order to receive VA health care and other benefits. Because of this restriction, once service members are discharged from the military, they are in a period of limbo where they are unable to receive care from either the DoD or the VA. This lag time is a potentially dangerous barrier to a patient's continuity of care as many injured service members are uninsurable because of their service-related injuries and may have to go without care if they are unable to afford health care independently.

Because DoD and VA disability boards have different purposes, disability ratings consistently vary between the two agencies. "While both the [services] and the VA use the VA Schedule for Rating Disabilities (VASRD), not all the general policy provisions set forth in the VASRD apply to the armed forces. Consequently, disability ratings may vary between the two agencies. The [military services] rate only conditions determined to be physically unfitting, compensating for loss of a military career. The VA may rate any service-connected impairment, thus compensating for loss of civilian employability."[29] Additionally, the term of rating is different between the Department of Defense and the Department of Veterans Affairs. While the Services' ratings are permanent once a final decision is made, VA ratings may fluctuate with time, depending upon the progression of the condition.[30]

Disability ratings also vary between the military services. According to the Independent Review Group, there is "widespread variance in the application of regulatory guidelines within each Service and between the Services. Variation continues at all levels of the disability process and into the Department of Veterans Affairs."[31] An Army Inspector General report found that the military's disability evaluation process failed to meet timeliness standards for determinations, employed inadequately trained staff in the evaluation process, and caused a great deal of confusion about the disability rating system among service members.[32]

It is this transition from the DoD medical system to the VA, with multiple disability evaluations and unnecessary restrictions preventing veterans from receiving VA care until in the VA system, that is the main impediment to veterans receiving proper, timely care. According to the Independent Review Group, "this needlessly cumbersome and perceived adversarial process is the center of gravity in the disability evaluation system and must be totally overhauled."[33]

In order to fix the problems resulting from these dual evaluations, the Independent Review Group recommended simplifying the process, "The Secretary of Defense, in conjunction with the Secretary of Veterans Affairs, should direct the transition process be streamlined for the service member separating from the Department of Defense and entering the Department of Veterans Affairs." According to Dole-Shalala, the DoD and the VA should work together to create a single, comprehensive, standardized medical examination that would serve both the DoD's purpose of determining fitness to serve and the VA's of determining initial disability level. Importantly, the DoD and the VA must implement the single physical exam as soon as possible.[34]

Adversarial and Outdated Disability Evaluations and Criteria

As outlined in the previous section, the DoD and the VA continue to face problems in providing a seamless transition of patient care from the time of a service member's injury until he or she is accepted into the VA. In many cases, the DoD and the VA's overlapping disability evaluation processes are the cause of disconnect. The nature of the evaluation processes themselves in both agencies, however, present further impediments to the delivery of health care and benefits that service members need and deserve. The two most common problems are a perceived adversarial DoD evaluation process and outdated VA disability evaluation criteria.

Adversarial DoD Evaluation Process

The Department of Defense's Physical Disability Evaluation System (PDES) is the "process for determining if active and reserve component members can reasonably perform the duties of their office, grade, rank or rating; AND if they are unable to perform the military duties because of a disease or injury that is service incurred or aggravated; AND if a disability rating for a lost military career should be assigned."[35]

The PDES includes the Medical Evaluation Board (MEB), the Physical Evaluation Board (PEB), and the applicable Service appeals board review process. As noted in the previous section, the injured service member must navigate the military's PDES before he or she can access Department of Veteran's Affairs health care and benefits.

However, the PDES is seen as adversarial by many injured service members who seek a rating threshold that entitles them to lifetime benefits while the department's incentive is to keep the ratings, and hence the benefits, low.[36] Throughout the process, the burden of securing medical validation and getting paper work completed, including a 23-page application, falls primarily to the veteran (unlike systems in the United Kingdom, Australia, and New Zealand, where the government effectively accepts the veteran's claim prima facie).[37]

The Department of Defense's military health system has two primary missions: to enhance our nation's security by providing health support for the full range of military operations, and to sustain the health of all those entrusted to its care.[38] As the DoD is not in the business of providing long-term care to injured service-members, it should not be in the business of establishing disability ratings. Both Dole-Shalala and the Independent Review group recommended that only the VA establish disability ratings. According to Dole-Shalala's recommendation, the DoD would maintain the authority to determine a service member's fitness to serve and would maintain responsibility to provide payments for years served, while the VA alone would establish the disability rating, compensation and benefits.

However, the problem is that the VA has its own difficulties providing adequate, consistent, and timely disability decisions.

Outdated VA Disability Evaluation Criteria

The VA's Schedule for Rating Disabilities (VASRD) is codified in statute and serves as a guide for the evaluation of disabilities resulting from diseases or injuries incidental to military service.[39] There are evaluation criteria for each condition listed, with disability levels ranging between zero and 100 percent, generally in 10 percent increments, as appropriate to the severity of the condition. The VA's disability rating level's amount is linked to a monetary amount determined by Congress and comes at a flat rate.[40]

The VA disability rating process is deeply flawed. In fact, the basis for the current VARSD has not been significantly updated since its development in 1945. Moreover, the VA uses a completely different system for rating disabilities than standard diagnostic codes and tools that are currently used by non-military governmental agencies, private sector disability plans, and medical providers.[41]

During the course of its review, the Independent Review Group identified no less than five Government Accountability Office reports and one Presidential Task force report dating back to 2003 that noted serious deficiencies in the VA's disability evaluation system. After more than a decade of analysis, the Government Accountability Office found that:

> VA's and other federal disability programs have not been updated to reflect the current state of science, medicine, technology, and labor market conditions. More specifically, VA's rating schedule, upon which disability decisions are made, is based primarily on estimates made in 1945 about the effect of service-connected impairments on the average individual's ability to perform jobs requiring manual labor.[42]

According to the study of the Schedule for Rating Disabilities conducted for the Veterans Disability Commission by the Institute of Medicine (IOM), "the rating schedule contains a number of obsolete diagnostic categories, terms, tests, and procedures, and does not recognize many currently accepted diagnostic categories.... In other cases, the diagnostic categories are current but do not specify appropriate procedures to measure disability for the conditions."[43]

Dole-Shalala found that the VA's disability evaluation process does not include diagnostic criteria for the types of injuries commonly incurred by soldiers returning from the wars in Iraq and Afghanistan. The VA's rating schedule does not acknowledge the disabling impact of conditions such as PTSD, and the effect medical advances have on the prognosis for certain conditions such as serious burns and amputations.[44] Nor does it include diagnostic criteria for the types of injuries for which treatment and understanding are changing rapidly, such as Traumatic Brain Injury (TBI).

Additionally, VASRD is also highly technical and difficult for soldiers to comprehend. The VASRD is divided into 14 body systems, which incorporate approximately 700 codes that describe illness or injury symptoms and levels of severity. According to the Dole-Shalala Commission the vast majority of service members are unfamiliar with the disability evaluation system. Only 38 percent of active duty, 34 percent of reserve component, and 38 percent of retired/separated service members say that they are "very" or "somewhat" satisfied with the disability evaluation system.[45]

Confusion about the ranking system along with the fact that many veterans are not aware of services and benefits they have earned through their military service causes many to fall through the cracks as they transition out of military service.

Continuity of Care and Case Management

Once in the VA care system, veterans face further challenges in accessing VA care as a result of poor case management and continuity of care.

- **Case Management**—the process intended to assist returning service members with management of their clinical and non-clinical care through recovery, rehabilitation and reintegration into the community—was identified by all three presidential evaluation groups as a major impediment to veteran care. As the GAO found, "Case management is especially important for returning service members who must often visit numerous therapists, providers, and specialists, resulting in differing treatment plans."[46] Poor case management continues to be a barrier to veterans receiving proper care.
- **Continuity of Care**—a seamless transition of patient care and records between agencies, clinicians, programs, and transition from inpatient to outpatient care,[47] was also identified by all three commissions as another critical impediment to service members receiving proper and timely medical care.[48]

The most common forms of these disconnects occur during:

1. Transition from one clinician to another; and
2. Transition from inpatient to outpatient care.

Transition from one Clinician to Another

As with the transition from one government agency to another (from the DoD to the VA) the transfer of a patient's care "from one clinician. . .organizational program, or clinical service to another" often inhibits the ability of the VA to provide proper health services. According to service members interviewed by the Independent Review Group, it is not uncommon for soldiers to visit numerous therapists, providers and specialists while in inpatient and outpatient care. This constant shifting results in differing treatment plans, as well as frequent receipt of prescriptions for multiple medications.[49]

Transition from Inpatient to Outpatient Care

The transition of patient care from inpatient to outpatient care is another source of confusion and disconnect in what should be the seamless delivery of health care services. "While first class trauma care is provided from the time of injury, through the evacuation from the battlefield, to transport to a tertiary medical facility, and during inpatient hospitalization, and establishes a high standard of excellence in trauma care," the "breakdown in health services and care management occurs once the service member transitions from inpatient to outpatient status.[50]

Inadequate access to outpatient care in many parts of the country also inhibits proper care. As the Independent Review Group notes, today's "service members come from locations across the nation. Without standard clinical approaches and access to care for service members and their families, civilian and military providers have inconsistent capability to meet the needs of their patients."[51]

In order to fix the problems resulting from improper continuum of care and case management, a joint DoD- and VA-led Senior Oversight Committee recommended establishing Federal Recovery Coordinators (FRC)—care managers to provide a smooth transition for severely wounded combat veterans who would have significant problems navigating the VA bureaucracy by themselves. While recovery coordinators do "not directly provide care, (they) coordinate federal health care teams and private community resources to achieve the personal and professional goals of an individualized 'life map' or recovery plan developed with the service members or veterans who qualify for the federal recovery coordinator program."[52]

Additionally, the Dole-Shalala Commission recommended the creation of "a patient-centered Recovery Plan" for seriously injured[53] service members that "provides the right care and support at the right time in the right place." The Commission found that a corps of well-trained, highly skilled Recovery Coordinators must be swiftly developed to ensure prompt development and execution of the recovery plan.[54]

As a result of these recommendations, a Federal Recovery Coordinator (FRC) program was established in mid 2007. Despite the priority given to the program, it has still not been fully implemented, in spite of the fact that it was intended to be in place no later than October 15, 2007. The FRC has three major problems that prevent it from being fully implemented.

First, the number of Federal Coordinators at major military medical facilities is woefully inadequate. While the VA plans to hire more, the Department has only been able to field a total of nine federal recovery coordinators since the program's inception. There are two each at Walter Reed Army Medical Center in Washington, D.C; National Naval Medical Center in Bethesda, Md.; and at Brooke Army Medical Center in San Antonio. The Balboa Navy Medical Center in San Diego and the VA medical centers in Houston and Providence, R.I., have only one coordinator each.[55]

Second, the VA is having problems retaining medical care coordinators for severely injured combat veterans. In fact, four of the first eight employees have already been replaced. "VA officials and congressional aides, speaking on the condition of not being identified, said they knew that the jobs were going to be stressful—dealing with seriously ill or wounded combat veterans who have especially complex needs can be demanding—but no one anticipated such high turnover. 'There is something called compassion fatigue that affects caregivers and families, and I can see that being magnified for someone who feels responsible not just for one severely injured person but several,' said a senior VA official."[56]

Finally, according to Douglas B. Carmon, assistant vice president for Military and Veterans Initiatives at Easter Seals, the Federal Recovery Coordinator Program "does not extend to what is arguably the most critical phase of recovery—the full reintegration into the service member's home community. Service members returning to their home communities still need these types of support to successfully transition back into civilian life."[57]

The military services have begun to implement their own programs to address shortcomings in case management and continuity of care. The Army has begun developing Warrior Transition Units—a three tiered organizational structure for case management. Within each unit a service member is assigned to a) a primary care physician, b) a nurse care manager, and c) a military squad leader, who are meant to coordinate the management of a service member's recovery process. Like the Federal Recovery Coordinator Program, the Army's Warrior Transition Units have had mixed results.

According to the Government Accountability Office, the Warrior Transition Unit is significantly short of staff at several key Army facilities. As of its last evaluation in September of 2007, more than half (17) of the 32 units had less than 50 percent of staff in place in one or more critical positions. Consequently, "46 percent of the Army's returning service members who were eligible to be assigned to a unit had not been assigned, due in part to the staffing shortages."[58]

Unless these shortfalls are addressed, wounded service members will not receive seamless and timely care.

Inadequate Department of Defense and Department of Veterans Affairs Information Sharing

Another factor that causes confusion between the DoD and the VA are the problems stemming from their inability to readily exchange medical information and patient data. Both the DoD and the VA use electronic medical record systems, but the VA system—the Veterans Health Information Systems and Technology Architecture (VHISTA)—and the DoD system (AHLTA) are not compatible for sharing electronic records.[59] This inability to communicate effectively continues to adversely affect the exchange of patient information between the two agencies.

For over a decade, the VA and DoD have been pursuing ways to share health information and to create comprehensive electronic medical records. The problem has been recognized for some time: in 2001 President Bush established the Task Force to Improve Health Care Delivery for Our Nation's Veterans. One of the task force's key recommendations, which stipulated that by 2005 the VA and DoD "should develop and deploy electronic medical records that are interoperable, bidirectional, and standards-based," has still not been implemented.[60]

Moreover, Dole-Shalala, the Task Force on Returning Global War on Terror Heroes, and the Veterans' Disability Benefits Commission Report, all recognized the continuing existence and the severity of this problem since 2007. Despite broad recognition of the problem, the actions taken to implement recommendations have not been adequate. Dole-Shalala noted that the DoD and VA "must move quickly to get clinical and benefit data to users, including making patient data immediately viewable by any provider, allied health professional, or program administrator who needs the data."[61]

The Senior Oversight Committee, a joint VA-DoD committee that was created in the wake of the Walter Reed scandal to manage the implementation of Dole-Shalala's recommendations, approved a requirement mandating that the DoD and VA make available all essential health and administrative data and that the information be viewable by both agencies. GAO notes that the departments are achieving only incremental increases to data sharing capabilities.

As recently as late April 2008, however, the GAO found that, "outpatient pharmacy and drug allergy data, but not other health care data, are currently electronic, interoperable, bidirectional, and standards-based . . . The departments are not able to exchange all health care data as computable medical records . . . as recommended by [the President's 2001] Task Force. Further, they have not developed a comprehensive plan with a completion date, which would guide the efforts until the goal of the comprehensive, seamless exchange of electronic medical records is achieved."[62]

The fact that both the problem and the solution to the DoD and VA file sharing difficulties have been recognized for some time but have yet to be addressed is additional evidence that the bureaucracy of both departments still remain on peacetime footings. This mindset must be changed in order to address this persistent problem.

Veterans Benefit Administration Claims Backlog

The Department of Veterans Affairs is plagued by a large and grow-ing claims backlog and will continue to face challenges processing the thousands of additional claims it is receiving every year. Specifically, the greatest challenges remain in speeding up the process of deciding claims, reducing the number of claims pending, and improving the accuracy and consistency of decisions across regional offices.[63] A number of factors are contributing to this increase in the inventory of pending claims, the in-ability to process them in a timely manner as well as the average time pending. These factors include:

1. Claims Volume
2. Increased VA Outreach
3. Increased Complexity of Claims Filed

As a consequence of these three factors, the VA's inventory of pending claims rose from nearly 579,000 in fiscal year 2000 to about 838,000 in fiscal year 2007, an increase of about 45 percent. In addition, VA projects that claims receipts will increase to about 872,000 in fiscal year 2009 and has warned that ongoing hostilities in Afghanistan and Iraq, and the Global War on Terror in general, may further increase its workload.[64]

Claims Volume

The major contributing factor to today's claims backlog is the sheer num-ber of claims currently being filed. According to the Government Account-ability Office, between fiscal years 2003 and 2007, the inventory of claims awaiting a decision grew by more than 50 percent to a total of about 392,000. Due to this influx, over the same period, the average number of days these claims were pending increased from 21 days, to an average of 132 days. Dur-ing the same period, the number of claims pending longer than 6 months more than doubled, increasing from about 47,000 to about 101,000.

Increased VA Outreach

The VA's outreach to veterans has increased dramatically the number of claims being filed as well as pending claims. The VA reports that in fis-cal year 2006, it provided benefits briefings to about 393,000 separating service members, up from about 210,000 in fiscal year 2003. As a result, the VA noted that the number of veterans receiving compensation has in-creased by about a half million between fiscal years 2000 to 2007.[65]

The Veterans Health Care Authorization Act, also known as the Fein-gold-Sanders bill, approved in June 2008, will extend the VA's outreach to recent veterans even further. This outreach improvement act expanded a grant program for community-based organizations to include state and local entities, including the National Guard and veteran service officers who conduct outreach for veterans.[66]

The VA's renewed push is already beginning to be felt. Spending on mental health programs throughout the VA system of medical centers, community clinics and vet centers will reached more than $3.5 billion in 2008 alone, and grow to $3.9 billion in 2009. Additionally, the VA is reaching out to more than 500,000 combat vets from the Global War on Terror who have not yet come to the VA for care and is notifying them of their benefits. Meanwhile, the VA vet center program is expanding with 23 new sites this year alone. This will bring the total around the country to 232.

Increased Complexity of Claims

Additionally, the increased complexity of cases being filed with the VA today is having a dramatic impact on the time it takes to process claims and the resulting claims backlog. According to a recent Government Accountability audit:

> Veterans are citing more disabilities in their claims than in the past and these claims can take longer to complete because each disability needs to be evaluated separately. *VA reported that the number of cases with eight or more disabilities claimed increased by 168 percent*—from about 21,800 to about 58,500—from 2000 to 2007. Additionally, VA notes that it is receiving claims for new and complex disabilities related to combat and deployments overseas, including those based on environmental and infectious disease risks and traumatic brain injuries. Further, VA reports receiving increasing numbers of claims for compensation for PTSD, which is generally more difficult to evaluate, in part because of the evidence required to link the disorder to a particular event.[67]

The majority of today's returning veterans are citing multiple heath problems, or what is known as "polytrauma." The average claim filed today cites five separate disabling medical conditions, while one in four returning veterans has applied for compensation for more than eight separate disabling conditions.[68]

Should one or more of the claims veterans file be denied by the VA, the veteran must then take his or her denied claim or claims to a VA appellate board where they face even more delays. According to Paul Sullivan, a former VA employee now with the non-profit veterans outreach group

Veterans for Common Sense, the appellate boards add exponentially to the time it takes to resolve a claim. "Our projection," said Sullivan in a recent interview, "is that it takes 12 to 15 years for a PTSD claim to work its way through the entire system, assuming initial denial. 12 to 15 years. Well, what happens? Most of these guys die or they give up somewhere along the line. You can't keep going that long."[69]

The long waiting lists, backlog, and time involved in appealing a decision are both frustrating and discouraging impediments to veteran patients looking to receive proper and timely health care and benefits. Anecdotal evidence indicates the effect the backlog has on our returning service members. For example: 41-year-old Steve Edwards, an Iraq war veteran, explained the effect of the VA claims problems in a recent interview with Australian Television. Edwards believes that the VA system is failing his army colleagues, "there's so many hoops and red tape to deal with that people just get fed up and walk away from (the VA health care system)."[70]

The VA and the Bush administration finally recognized the escalating claims problem and began hiring new employees to handle the mounting claims. The President's Fiscal Year 2009 budget request called for an increase of over 2,600 full-time equivalent employees from actual fiscal year 2007 levels to process compensation claims. All together, the fiscal year 2009 request would fund approximately 11,000 total full-time equivalent employees working on compensation and pension claims, an increase of 32 percent over fiscal year 2007.[71]

While welcome, these additions are little more than a Band-Aid on the problem. According to Stiglitz and Bilmes, "without a major overhaul of the current system, veterans are virtually guaranteed bigger claims backlogs, longer waiting lists, and possible diminished quality of medical care. The hundreds of thousands of new veterans who seek medical care and disability compensation in the next few years will overwhelm the system in terms of scheduling, diagnostic testing, claims evaluation, and access to specialists in such areas as traumatic brain injury."[72]

The impediments to care at the VA are a result of its culture as well as its operation. While interviewing a VA employee who asked to remain anonymous regarding the link between claims backlogs and delayed patient benefits, the employee asserted, "see that's where you are mistaken, that is VBA (Veterans Benefit Administration), not 'big VA' (the Department of Veterans Affairs proper)." Only when asked if the VBA backlog affects the time it takes for a veteran's claim to be processed in order to receive VA benefits did the employee acknowledge that, indeed, the problems were linked.

There remain two ways to address this monumental and expanding VA health care crisis: either address each problem piecemeal and enact marginal reforms until the next crisis comes, or enact a complete DoD-VA-wide overhaul. As one anonymous VA employee interviewed for this chapter said, "The (VA health care) system is a system built in 1945 to address the problems and injuries of returning white male soldiers from World War II. Since then, there has been regulation, on top of regulation, on top of regulation, but the system fails to properly address the unique needs of today's returning soldiers. In my opinion, the system needs to be blown up and we need to start over again."

Our nation's veterans deserve a better system of care than the one that is in place today; one that is tailored to the needs of today's returning veterans, one that enables injured military people to increase their chances for recovery and their opportunity to return to a normal life. As the preceding sections demonstrated, the problems with the VA health care system are interconnected and are best addressed by enacting comprehensive reform.

As mentioned before, the signature injuries of the wars in Iraq and Afghanistan, namely Posttraumatic Stress Disorder (PTSD) and Traumatic Brain Injury (TBI) have created a large claims backlog for the VA. The inherent complexity and sheer number of the psychological and cognitive injuries coming out of these conflicts will challenge the VA for years to come. Indeed, a discussion of the signature injuries of the wars in Iraq and Afghanistan is essential to confront the multiple epidemics plaguing the VA today and that will continue to plague it in the future.

Notes

1. Congressional Budget Office, "The Healthcare System for Veterans: An Interim Report," December 2007, Preface, http://cbo.gov/ftpdocs/88xx/doc8892/12-21-VA_Healthcare.pdf.

2. Department of Veterans Affairs, "FY 07 VA Information Pamphlet," http://www1.va.gov/vetdata/docs/Pamphlet_2-1-08.pdf.

3. Congressional Budget Office, "The Healthcare System for Veterans," 1.

4. Department of Veterans Affairs, "FY 07 VA Information Pamphlet."

5. Phillip Longman, "The Best Care Anywhere," *Washington Monthly*, January/February 2005, http://www.washingtonmonthly.com/features/2005/0501.longman.html#byline.

6. Congressional Budget Office, "The Healthcare System for Veterans," 10.

7. Department of Veterans Affairs, "Report to the Appropriations Committee of the U.S. House of Representatives in response to House Appropriations Report No. 110–186, accompanying Public Law 110–161, The Consolidated Appropriations Act, 2008," 5–6, http://www1.va.gov/health/docs/Hospital_Quality_Report.pdf.

8. Ibid.

9. Phillip Longman, "The Best Care Anywhere."

10. Joseph Stiglitz and Linda Bilmes, *The Three Trillion Dollar War: The True Cost of the Iraq Conflict* (New York: W. W. Norton, 2008), 81.

11. Veterans Benefit Commission, "Chapter 3: Veterans' Past, Present and Future," 44 http://www.vetscommission.org/pdf/Veterans_Past_Present_Future-ch-3.pdf.

12. Department of Veterans Affairs, "FY 07 VA Information Pamphlet."

13. Department of Veterans Affairs, "FY 07 VA Information Pamphlet."

14. Stiglitz and Bilmes, *The Three Trillion Dollar War,* 85 (emphasis added).

15. Department of Veterans Affairs, Enrollment Priority Groups, http://www.va.gov/healtheligibility/eligibility/PriorityGroups.asp.

16. RAND Corporation, "Invisible Wounds of War," 268, http://www.rand.org/pubs/monographs/2008/RAND_MG720.pdf.

17. Stiglitz and Bilmes, *The Three Trillion Dollar War,* 64.

18. RAND, "Invisible Wounds of War," 301.

19. Stiglitz and Bilmes, *The Three Trillion Dollar War,* 82.

20. Data provided by Veterans for Common Sense, July 2008.

21. Department of Veterans Affairs Office of the Inspector General, "Audit of the Veterans Health Administration's Outpatient Waiting Time," i, September 10, 2007, http://www.va.gov/oig/52/reports/2007/vaoig-07-00616-199.pdf.

22. Ibid., 5.

23. Ibid., 8 (emphasis added).

24. Ibid., 7.

25. Ibid., 19.

26. Report on the Rehabilitative Care and Administrative Processes at Walter Reed Army Medical Center and National Naval Medical Center, 9, http://nationalsecurity.oversight.house.gov/documents/20070418170543.pdf.

27. Stiglitz and Bilmes, *The Three Trillion Dollar War,* 68.

28. Government Accountability Office, "DoD and VA: Preliminary Observations on Efforts to Improve Health Care and Disability Evaluations for Returning Servicemembers," September 26, 2007, http://www.gao.gov/new.items/d071256t.pdf (emphasis added).

29. United States Army, "Veterans Administration Schedule for Rating Disabilities (VASRD) Fact Sheet," http://myarmybenefits.us.army.mil/EN/Benefits/FactSheets/VASRD.Codes/FactSheet.aspx?articleId=6655c6d9a15f4ea3972fa1b95f086ff3.

30. Ibid.

31. Report on the Rehabilitative Care and Administrative Processes at Walter Reed Army Medical Center and National Naval Medical Center, 28.

32. Office of the Inspector General, Department of the Army, Report on the Army Physical Disability Evaluation System, March 6, 2007, http://www.army.mil/institution/operations/reports/IGReport-APDESI/IG%20Report%20-%20Army%20Physical%20Disability%20Evaluation%20System%20Inspection.pdf.

33. Report on the Rehabilitative Care and Administrative Processes at Walter Reed Army Medical Center and National Naval Medical Center, 28.

34. Report of the President's Commission on Care for America's Returning Wounded Warriors, 7, http://www.veteransforamerica.org/wp-content/uploads/2008/12/presidents-commission-on-care-for-americas-returning-wounded-warriors-report-july-2007.pdf.

35. Report on the Rehabilitative Care and Administrative Processes at Walter Reed Army Medical Center and National Naval Medical Center, 28.

36. Government Accountability Office, "DoD and VA: Preliminary Observations on Efforts to Improve Health Care and Disability Evaluations for Returning Service Members," September 26, 2007.

37. Stiglitz and Bilmes, *The Three Trillion Dollar War,* 69.

38. RAND, "Invisible Wounds of War," 253.

39. Report on the Rehabilitative Care and Administrative Processes at Walter Reed Army Medical Center and National Naval Medical Center, 31.

40. Task Force on Returning Global War on Terror Heroes, 22, http://www1.va.gov/taskforce/docs/Section4_GWOTTF.pdf.

41. House Committee on Veterans Affairs, "VA Disability Rating System in Need of Comprehensive and Immediate Repair," http://veterans.house.gov/news/PRArticle.aspx?NewsID=206.

42. Government Accountability Office, "Veterans' Disability Benefits: Processing of Claims Continues to Present Challenges," March 13, 2007, 2, http://www.gao.gov/new.items/d07562t.pdf.

43. Veterans Benefit Commission, "Chapter 4: Ratings Process and System," 71, http://www.vetscommission.org/pdf/Rating_Process_and_System-ch-4.pdf.

44. Government Accountability Office, "Veterans' Disability Benefits Claims Processing Challenges Persist, while VA Continues to Take Steps to Address them," February 14, 2008, 10, http://www.gao.gov/new.items/d08473t.pdf.

45. Report of the President's Commission on Care for America's Returning Wounded Warriors, 6.

46. Government Accountability Office, "DoD and VA: Preliminary Observations on Efforts to Improve Health Care and Disability Evaluations for Returning Service Members," September 26, 2007.

47. Report on the Rehabilitative Care and Administrative Processes at Walter Reed Army Medical Center and National Naval Medical Center, 12.

48. Ibid.

49. Ibid.

50. Ibid., 3.

51. Ibid., 19.

52. Department of Veterans Affairs, "VA-DoD Program Serves Severely Disabled Combat Veterans," May 7, 2008, http://www1.va.gov/opa/pressrel/pressrelease.cfm?id=1499.

53. The Dole-Shalala Commission defined a serious injury as a physiological condition affecting one or more body systems that has lasted or is expected to last at least 12 continuous months and that precludes unaided performance of at least one major life activity (breathing, cognition, hearing, seeing, ability to bathe, dress, eat, groom, speak, use stairs or toiler, transfer, walk).

54. Report of the President's Commission on Care for America's Returning Wounded Warriors, 5.

55. Rick Maze, "VA Losing Care Coordinators," *Air Force Times,* June 27, 2008, http://www.airforcetimes.com/news/2008/06/military_va_recoverycoordinators_062708w/.

56. Ibid.

57. Testimony of Douglas B. Carmon before the U.S. Senate Committee on Veterans' Affairs, February 5, 2008, http://frwebgate.access gpo.gov/cgi-bin/getdoc.cgi?dbname=110_senate_hearings&docid=f:41914.wais.

58. Government Accountability Office, "Preliminary Observations on Efforts to Improve Health Care and Disability Evaluations for Returning Service Members," September 26, 2007, 11.

59. RAND, "Invisible Wounds of War," 272.

60. Government Accountability Office, "Computer Based Patient Records," 3, http://www.gao.gov/new.items/d04402t.pdf.

61. Government Accountability Office, "DoD and VA: Preliminary Observationson Efforts to Improve Health Care and Disability Evaluations For Returning Servicemembers," September 26, 2007, http://www.gao.gov/new.items/d071256t.pdf.

62. Government Accountability Office, "VA and DoD Health Care: Progress Made on Implementation of 2003 President's Task Force Recommendations on Collaboration and Coordination, but More Remains to Be Done," April 30 2008, 7, http://www.gao.gov/new.items/d08495r.pdf.

63. Government Accountability Office, "Veterans' Disability Benefits: Claims Processing Challenges Persist, while VA Continues to Take Steps to Address Them," February 14, 2008, 1.

64. Ibid., 5.

65. Ibid., 5.

66. Senate Press Release, "Senate Committee Passes Feingold, Sanders Effort to Expand Outreach to Veterans," June 27, 2008, http://feingold.senate.gov/~feingold/releases/08/06/20080626v.html.

67. Government Accountability Office, "Veterans' Disability Benefits: Claims Processing Challenges Persist," 6 (emphasis added).

68. Stiglitz and Bilmes, *The Three Trillion Dollar War,* 66

69. Nick Lazaredes, "America's Forgotten Soldiers," SBS Dateline, http://www.gsfso.org/Forgotten_Soldiers-US_Veterans.html.

70. Ibid.

71. Government Accountability Office, "Veterans' Disability Benefits," 7.

72. Stiglitz and Bilmes, *The Three Trillion Dollar War,* 88.

CHAPTER 6

Multiple Epidemics in Veteran Mental Health

Sean E. Duggan

Throughout American history, various labels have been attached to returning service members who experience mental health problems and depression resulting from the pressures of combat environments—the so-called invisible wounds of war. Although different labels have been applied over the years, "soldiers' heart" in the Civil War, "shell shock" in World War I, and "battle fatigue" in World War II, all the terms essentially described the same condition. Yet, as discussed in Chapter 2, it was not until after the Vietnam War that a broad recognition of the symptoms and causes of what has become known as Posttraumatic Stress Disorder (PTSD) became widely recognized.

Psychological disorders resulting from the extreme pressures and stressful environments of combat, as discussed in Chapter 4, are hardly unique to the wars in Iraq and Afghanistan. However, several aspects of both wars—tough grinding counterinsurgency warfare, close urban combat, and repeated and lengthy deployments characterized by short dwell times between deployments—have all contributed to the wide-spread prevalence of PTSD in today's returning service members.

Growing acceptance and recognition of PTSD and its related effects within the military and civilian society have also led to the dramatic increase in PTSD awareness and diagnosis. Whereas seeking help for PTSD-related symptoms was once grounds for ridicule, career stagnation, and in some cases punishment, the military has undertaken a concerted effort to reduce the stigma surrounding the disorder. While anecdotal evidence suggests that the stigma has hardly disappeared from contemporary military culture, today's environment is much more conducive to military people seeking help than it has been in previous wars.

PTSD, however, is only one of the signature injuries of the wars in Iraq and Afghanistan. Traumatic Brain Injuries (TBI), cognitive dysfunctions resulting from an extreme external force, are also increasingly common in today's returning service members. Just as the grueling environments of Iraq and Afghanistan magnify the effects of PTSD, the signature weapons of the wars in Iraq and Afghanistan—extremely high powered explosives and electrically formed penetrators—multiply the instances of TBI.

According to the Independent Review Group, as many as "one-fourth of all returning service members, from Operation Enduring Freedom and Operation Iraqi Freedom, are struggling" with these less visible injuries.[1] These service members report exposure to multiple life-changing stressors during their wartime experience.

But despite widespread policy interest and a firm commitment from the DoD and the VA to address these injuries, according to a landmark study released by the RAND Corporation in mid-2008 "fundamental gaps remain in our knowledge about the mental health and cognitive needs of U.S. service members returning from Afghanistan and Iraq, the adequacy of the care systems available to meet those needs, the experience of veterans and service members who are in need of services, and factors related to whether and how injured service members and veterans seek care."[2]

In order to correct the multiple epidemics in mental health confronting today's returning veterans, these issues must be addressed head on. PTSD and TBI, however, are not the only hardships facing service members upon their return home. As the Independent Review Group documents, the effects of PTSD and TBI "often challenge [service members'] ability to easily reintegrate to family and peacetime life following deployment. 'Survival strategies', which are highly adaptive in a combat environment, are often disruptive to civilian life; interpersonal and family functioning is inevitably affected by combat exposure."[3]

As a result of their PTSD and TBI symptoms, large and growing numbers of returning service members are also dealing with substance abuse problems. These problems often develop as troops seek short-term cures to their PTSD symptoms and other emotional and cognitive disorders. Often, these substance abuse problems end up fueling interpersonal and family problems that in turn exacerbate their substance abuse problems and TBI/PTSD symptoms in a vicious cycle.

The VA must continue to recognize the scope of the large and growing PTSD/TBI problem; continue to address the gaps in availability and quality of care for service members suffering from these disorders; and be prepared to mitigate the effects they are having upon service members' lives as they return home—specifically substance abuse problems, suicide attempts, spousal abuse and homelessness.

Posttraumatic Stress Disorder (PTSD)

Scope of the Problem

The scope of the PTSD problem is immense. While the VA is currently treating over 100,000 veterans from the wars in Iraq and Afghanistan who exhibit PTSD symptoms, the actual number of service members from Iraq and Afghanistan suffering from PTSD is likely much higher. According to the RAND study, approximately 300,000 returning service members from Iraq and Afghanistan could be suffering from PTSD or major depression.[4]

While it is difficult to summarize the many symptoms of PTSD, several studies have attempted to offer a comprehensive diagnosis. According to the Independent Review Group, Posttraumatic Stress Disorder "is one of a range of deployment-related psychological effects of war. The diagnostic criteria include: (1) the person should have been exposed to a traumatic event; (2) the trauma is re-experienced in one of a number of ways, including dreams and flashbacks; (3) there is a persistent avoidance of traumatic stimuli; (4) there is increased arousal; and (5) the duration is longer than a month."

The costs associated with PTSD and related clinical depression are also enormous. The National Institute of Medicine has found that while PTSD accounts for only 8.7 percent of total disability claims, it represents a disproportionate 20.5 percent of compensation benefit payments.[5] According to RAND, "two-year costs associated with PTSD are approximately $5,904 to $10,298, depending on whether we include the cost of lives lost to suicide. Two-year costs associated with major depression are approximately $15,461 to $25,757, and costs associated with co-morbid PTSD and major depression are approximately $12,427 to $16,884."[6] When multiplied by the potential number service members experiencing PTSD symptoms, the costs associated with PTSD in the coming decades will be in the hundreds of billions of dollars.

Today's Multiple and Prolonged Deployments

Although the effect of multiple and prolonged deployments on service members' mental health was examined in some detail in Chapter 4, it is important to summarize both factors again in this section because of the impact that the length and frequency of today's deployments are having on service members' mental health.

According to a report issued in early 2008 by the Office of the Surgeon General for the United States Army Medical Command (MHAT V) both factors have a significant impact on soldiers' mental health.

> *Multiple Deployments.* Soldiers on their third or fourth deployment were at significantly higher risk than Soldiers on their first or second deployment for mental health problems and work-related problems. A Non-Commissioned Officer (NCO) on his or her second or third/fourth deployment reports significantly more mental health problems (adjusted percent of 27.2%) than does an NCO on his or her second deployment (adjusted percent of 18.5%) and significantly more than an NCO on his or her first deployment (adjusted percent of 11.9%).[7]

> *Deployment Length.* Reports of work-related problems due to stress, mental health problems and marital separations generally increased with each subsequent month of the deployment. Behavioral health results suggest that the post six-month period is a heightened risk time for mental health problems and that reports of mental health problems level off in the months immediately before redeployment (possibly due to anticipation of returning home). Nonetheless, the adjusted percent of Soldiers reporting mental health problems at month 15 is significantly higher than the percent reporting problems in the early months, and redeployment research strongly suggests that rates will rise when [the] Soldier return[s].[8]

Delayed Onset of PTSD

The nature of PTSD's delayed onset contributes to the current underestimation of the looming PTSD problem. In a recent study conducted by the U.S. Army, only four to five percent of soldiers were referred to mental health care based upon their first Post-Deployment Health Assessment, but at the second assessment conducted three to six months later, the figure jumped to 20.3 percent for active duty soldiers and a staggering 42.4 percent for soldiers from the reserve component (Army National Guard and Army Reserves).[9]

In the second assessment, symptoms for PTSD jumped by 40 percent from 11.8 percent to 16.7 percent; clinical depression more than doubled from 4.7 percent to 10.3 percent; issues relating to interpersonal conflict experienced a four-fold increase from 3.5 percent to 14.0 percent; and overall mental health issues increased by 60 percent from 17.0 percent to 27.1 percent.[10]

Those troops who have been seriously injured are more likely to develop PTSD and depression over time. Rates of depression and PTSD among severely wounded service members increased significantly between the initial 1-month post-injury assessment (where 4.2% had PTSD symptoms and 4.4% had depression) to seven months post-injury (where 12.0% had PTSD and 9.3% met criteria for depression).[11]

While the reasons for this delayed onset are numerous, Jim Dooley, a VA Mental Health counselor, put it well when he said, "when soldiers return, they begin to struggle internally with what they experienced, what they did, and what they didn't do. When you're finally back (home) and you finally make connection with your safety, which is your family that's when you begin to vibrate with the fact of where you were. Now you can actually acknowledge how scared you were. This is the most damaging type of war, psychologically, you have no protection anywhere, at all times. And therefore you are in constant death threat. You are also witnessing death at incredibly close range and you are witnessing the carnage."[12]

In an effort to identify all returning service members who may exhibit PTSD symptoms, the military currently conducts two PTSD screenings: The Post-Deployment Health Assessment (PDHA) immediately after a deployment, and a Post-Deployment Health Reassessment (PDHRA) six months after a deployment.

1. "The Department of Defense uses the PDHA to screen service members at the end of a deployment outside the United States. The questionnaire includes a specific four-item screen for posttraumatic stress disorder. The four questions cover key domains of posttraumatic stress disorder, including re-experiencing trauma, numbing, avoidance and hyperarousal."[13]
2. "The Department of Defense uses the PDHRA questionnaire [to reassess] service members' physical and mental health three to six months following the member's return from a deployment outside the United States. This reassessment offers service members time to be with their families and to begin readjustment. The timing of this reassessment allows service members to identify issues that, if identified earlier, [might] have kept them from joining their families right away. This reassessment involves all health issues; since the focus does not specify mental health issues, it minimizes stigma."[14]

Problems with the PDHA and PDHRA

While both post-deployment screenings for PTSD symptoms are necessary, both have their limitations. First, the timing of the initial PDHA does not provide a reliable screening. A number of studies have shown that service members say they do not always report mental health concerns immediately after deployments because they fear that doing so might delay their return home.[15] Anecdotal evidence also suggests the timing does not lend itself to proper identification of PTSD symptoms. According to Cpl.

Dan Gay, a recently returned marine interviewed by PBS's *Frontline,* "We had questionnaires, and the standard, 'If you have any problems write them down now and we'll keep you here and we'll study 'em until we figure out whether you're better or not. You just want to go home. Nobody wants to sit there and say, 'Yeah, I don't sleep so good anymore…or something like that. Generally speaking you just say, 'I'm a-ok' and you just want to go home and see your family."[16]

Second, the PDHA is a self-screening and is not conducted by a health care professional. Consequently, returning service members are not thoroughly examined for PDST symptoms and merely have to fill out a form upon their return home. According to Sergeant Roy Meredith, team leader of the Maryland Army National Guard, in recent testimony before the Senate Veterans' Affairs Committee, "the PDHA provides an early opportunity to assess the physical condition of soldiers. This is great because the goal should be to identify and capture any condition as soon as possible. However, unlike the pre-mobilization physical assessment, the PDHA is not a complete physical but based on self identification of ailments."

Third, while the second screening, the PDHRA, is a necessary follow-up given service members' understandable desire simply to "go home" after a deployment and given the delayed onset of PTSD symptoms, it too has a number of flaws. According to Sergeant Roy Meredith, the PDHRA "lacks the key strengths that support an effective PDHA: control and access to the soldiers. From what I have seen, as soldiers return to their homes, it is difficult to communicate and require them to attend PDHRA events. I think the primary reason for this breakdown relates to the fact that members are not provided military orders requiring them to report."[17]

National Guard and Reserve Soldiers Are More Susceptible to PTSD

According to a recent study conducted by Dr. Joseph Scotti, veterans who deployed as members of the National Guard and Reserves are experiencing a greater negative impact on psychological and daily functioning than veterans who served while on active duty.

Dr. Scotti's study, conducted on 848 active duty National Guard, and reserve service members from West Virginia, found that members of the Guard/Reserves are more likely than active duty personnel to meet the criteria for PTSD/Depression (51% vs. 40%), despite having similar demographic backgrounds and combat experiences. Higher levels of PTSD symptoms were also found in reserve component soldiers in the study conducted by the U.S. Army.

This result may reflect the impact of predeployment preparation and training, support of families during deployment, and postdeployment debriefing and support resources. According to Scotti, the differences in the intensity, regularity, and type of training between active military and National Guard units may also play a factor.[18]

Gaps in Access and Quality of Care for PTSD

As discussed in Chapter 5, many of the gaps in access and quality of care that veterans face when seeking treatment for their PTSD symptoms also exist in the civilian health care system. In this sense, many of these gaps are not just a VA problem so much as a deficiency in the American health care system in general. Nonetheless, these gaps must be understood and corrected if service members are to receive proper treatment.

The VA has made a concerted effort to adapt to the mental health care needs of incoming veterans. Among other notable efforts, the Veterans Affairs' National Center for PTSD reports that each VA Medical Center offers some type of specialized expertise with PTSD, resulting in a network of more than 200 specialized treatment programs and trauma centers.[19]

Despite the VA's commendable efforts, many serious deficiencies remain. According to RAND, the magnitude of the challenges in improving care for mental health conditions and TBI for service members should not be underestimated. The Government Accountability Office notes that, "While DoD and VA are considered leaders in PTSD research and treatment, knowledge generated through research and clinical experience is not systematically disseminated to all DoD and VA providers of care."[20] In addition to the problems in assessing and recognizing patients with PTSD, the VA is facing other problems: "obtaining qualified health professionals, such as clinical psychologists, is a challenge, which is due to competition with private sector salaries and difficulty recruiting for certain geographical locations."[21]

According to the Independent Review Group, this shortfall of both psychiatrists and psychologists is also prevalent in the military services. "In years past, there have been approximately 450 active duty licensed clinical psychologists serving their country in uniform. Today, that number has shrunk to less than 350 (a 22% decrease), and the rate of attrition continues at an alarming pace."[22]

Efforts to cure the problem by filling the gaps for psychiatric and psychological healthcare professionals both in the armed services and the VA will not be successful unless other impediments to care, namely social and cultural barriers, are also addressed. Surely, "expanding the number of mental health providers will not make care more accessible if the concerns about negative consequences associated with getting care are not alleviated."[23] It is therefore necessary to consider pervasive social and cultural barriers to care.

Social and Cultural Barriers to Veterans Seeking and Receiving PTSD Care

While the lack of qualified mental care professionals and unevenly disseminated expertise is a large impediment to proper and timely care, persistent social and cultural barriers can be an even greater deterrent. As noted above, while the stigma associated with mental health problems has declined in recent years, it is far from gone.

According to the RAND study, the most commonly perceived barriers to receiving mental health care among service members were: a fear of being seen as weak (65% of respondents); the fact that unit leadership might treat them differently (63% of respondents); a fear that members of their unit would have less confidence in them (61% of respondents); perceptions that seeking mental health care would harm their careers (51%); that service members saw seeking help as too embarrassing (42% of respondents); while many simply didn't trust mental health professionals (38% of respondents). Moreover, nearly half of the respondents said that they perceived the difficulty in scheduling an appointment to be a major barrier.

As a result of these social and cultural barriers, only 23–40 percent of military personnel, who met screening criteria post-deployment, received any professional help while significantly less, 13 to 27 percent, received care from mental health professionals. Additionally, only about half of OEF or OIF veterans with a referral for a mental health problem listed on the postdeployment health assessment used mental health services.[24]

While these results were obtained from service members, pervasive apprehensions rooted in the military's institutional culture—which emphasizes individual strength, toughness, and team effort—remain a barrier to veterans seeking personal mental heath care as well.

Denying the Problem Is Not a Solution

According to Gordon Erspamer, the lead lawyer representing Veterans for Common Sense and Veterans United for Truth in the recent landmark federal suit filed against the VA, the U.S. military has discharged tens of thousands of veterans on the basis of what the military claimed were pre-existing personality disorders. Even though these men and women are combat veterans, they essentially get no benefits at all.

> They're doing it just to get rid of people, to save money, so they don't have to pay them disability benefits and they don't have to pay them for the medical care. There's been...over 22,000 of those from Iraq and Afghanistan. I mean, we're not talking about small numbers. 22,000 people, this is another budgetary thing. Part of our case deals

with that issue and what we're asking the court to do is to tell the VA "Look, you can't rely on any of these personality disorder discharges. You've got to start from fresh with this veteran and decide do they have PTSD. If they do, is it service-connected, and give them benefits and ignore what the military did to them, because it's so unreliable."[25]

Minimizing the large and growing PTSD epidemic by discharging service members with potential PTSD symptoms before they can claim DoD and VA benefits is clearly not a solution, either legally and morally. As the VA has historically adapted its programs and treatment approaches to meet the changing mental health needs of returning troops,[26] it must continue to adapt in order to correct the current and future challenges presented by the many hundreds of thousands of incoming veterans dealing with PTSD.

Traumatic Brain Injury (TBI)

Scope of the Problem

Unlike PTSD, whose symptoms and treatment methods have been catalogued and studied since Vietnam, "currently, no standard administrative code exists for documenting mild traumatic brain injuries in the medical record." This lack of "documentation in medical records severely limits research and therefore, education efforts" in order to treat TBI.[27] Moreover, RAND found that there is limited research on the prevalence of traumatic brain injury, owing to assessment difficulties, case definitions, and restrictions on the release of such information.

Traumatic Brain Injury, however, is more prevalent in today's returning service members than PTSD. RAND found that as many as 320,000 service members from Iraq and Afghanistan are likely to have suffered TBI while deployed. The types of weapons used in both Iraq and Afghanistan, highly powerful explosives, the so-called Improvised Explosive Devices (IEDs) are primarily responsible for the large number of TBI injuries. In fact, nearly 65 percent of all service members wounded in action in Iraq have been injured in a blast injury, which often causes TBI.[28] As Stiglitz and Bilmes note:

These type of blasts create rapid pressure shifts, or blast waves, that can cause direct brain injuries such as concussion, contusion (injury in which the skin is not broken), and cerebral infarcts (areas of tissue that die as a result of a loss of blood supply). The blast waves also can blow fragments of metal or other matter into people's body or heads.

Today's troops wear Kevlar body armor and helmets, which reduce the frequency of penetrating head injuries but do not prevent the "closed" brain injuries produced by blasts.[29]

As noted in Chapter 4, due in large part to the number of troops surviving powerful blasts, TBI is very prevalent in today's returning troops. Where as in previous conflicts, the mortality rate from such injuries was 75 percent or higher, the majority of these troops are now being saved.[30]

In terms of financial costs, TBI greatly exceeds costs associated with treating PTSD. "One-year costs for service members who have accessed the health care system and received a diagnosis of traumatic brain injury…rang[e] from $25,572 to $30,730 in 2005 for mild cases…and from $252,251 to $383,221 for moderate or severe cases."[31]

Difficulties Identifying and Diagnosing TBI

Like PTSD, TBI has become known as an invisible wound because, in many cases, there is no way to readily identify those with the disorder while conducting a cursory physical examination. TBI is currently defined as "an acquired, external force upon the brain most often resulting in an alteration in consciousness at the time of injury, loss of memory around the event, and some level of cognitive dysfunction. It is possible to have a traumatic brain injury in the absence of any observable physical damage to the brain. Difficulties after a traumatic brain injury include headaches, sleep difficulties, decreased memory and attention, irritability, depression and slowed mental processing."[32]

There are "several methods used to scan for TBI, including computed tomography (CT), quantitative electroencephalography (QEEG), and magnetic resonance imaging (MRI), among others. MRIs are used most often in the military health care system, but among the various types of MRI (e.g., different sequencing, fast spin/slow spin, high resolution/low resolution, 2 Tesla/4.5 Tesla), there is a wide range of diagnostic accuracy. Indeed, it is common for some instances of mild TBI to be missed."[33]

In cases analyzed by Veterans for America, a non-partisan veterans research group in Washington, DC, it is clear that there is an inadequate application of the different scans, and their resulting images, for the treatment of service members suffering from mild forms of TBI. According to the VFA, "Scans are used to determine the presence or absence of TBI, after which a predetermined regimen of treatments is prescribed. The stated position of the U.S. military is that anyone who requests a TBI scan or who shows symptoms of TBI will receive an MRI. However, VFA has observed a wide range of accessibility issues that reduce the effectiveness of this policy, including long wait times for a scan and the willingness of primary care providers to refer a service member for scanning."[34] As a result, when service members separate from the military and enter the VA system, many cases of mild TBI are not identified.

Further complicating the ability of the DoD and VA to identify cases of TBI resulting from a battlefield injury is the fact that events that cause TBI are often not recorded on the battlefield. To address the problem, Army Brigadier General Michael Tucker, deputy commander of Walter Reed Army Medical Center, announced in early 2007 (four years into the Iraq war and over five years into the war in Afghanistan) that he was recommending that the Army begin comprehensively gathering TBI-related information on the battlefield. As the VFA points out, "unfortunately, the absence of such efforts in the past has impeded treatment and complicated the disability rating process, placing the onus on the service member to prove that wounds are combat-related. In short, many service members have suffered mild TBIs but have not been diagnosed with this injury...The burden of proof is on the service member to review his or her combat records and make the case that the injury occurred in the line of duty, a burden many are not able to bear because of their injury."[35]

Perhaps the greatest impediment to identifying a battle-related TBI is the fact that many troops who have been deployed numerous times to the wars in Iraq and Afghanistan were never screened with brain-function tests before their deployments. The "Army did not establish a baseline of brain functioning before troops were deployed the first time. Without such a record, it is impossible to precisely say when a soldier endured TBI."[36] One healthcare professional, formerly employed by the military, put it well when she said, "without a predeployment baseline to reference against, establishing whether or not a service member incurred a Traumatic Brain Injury while on duty is significantly more difficult to assess. It is like reading the end of a book and trying to figure out how it began."[37]

The Army has begun preliminary efforts to address these shortcomings. Fort Campbell in Kentucky, for example, has made it mandatory that soldiers undergo brain-function tests before they redeploy to Iraq and Afghanistan, while those deploying from Fort Bragg in North Carolina are given the option to take the test.[38] However, to ensure that the DoD and VA are able to identify and treat TBI properly, Veterans for America has called on the DoD to institute a Department-wide policy that no soldier or marine will be deployed until a baseline brain function is established. Moreover, to ensure that service members are not suffering from undiagnosed mild TBIs, Veterans for America called on the DoD to have trained professionals conduct face-to-face screenings of all service members who have served—and are serving—in Iraq and Afghanistan.[39]

Gaps in Access and Quality of Care for TBI

Aside from the gaps in care that result from the difficulties in identifying and diagnosing TBI listed above, there remain other impediments to proper care for TBI. The Independent Review Group found that while "many good people are doing a lot of good work regarding traumatic brain injury at many levels and many locations, *it is neither coordinated nor consistent*. Although the Department of Defense and Department of Veterans Affairs established one central body, the Defense and Veterans Brain Injury Center (DVBIC), there is lack of penetration, system-wide, to affect an effective definition, clinical guidelines, and treatment to the scale required for returning service members and veterans."[40]

Moreover, while "the Defense and Veterans Brain Injury Center provides information on traumatic brain injury care and offers educational material for providers and family members…their findings…are not reaching the entire system and are not universally applied."[41]

As noted above, the effects of PTSD and TBI "often challenge (service members') ability to reintegrate successfully to family and peacetime life following deployment. 'Survival strategies', which are highly adaptive in a combat environment, are often disruptive to civilian life; interpersonal and family functioning is inevitably affected by combat exposure."[42]

Indeed, the rise of PTSD and TBI injuries has led to other crises in troops' lives upon their return home, as witnessed by higher suicide rates, higher substance abuse rates, and the higher numbers of veterans becoming homeless relatively soon after being discharged.

Conclusion

Long-Term Outlook

Over $43 billion, or half of the Department of Veterans Affairs' budget in Fiscal Year 2007 (nearly $86 billion that year), was paid directly to the current veteran population—those veterans of previous conflicts and veterans of the wars in Iraq and Afghanistan who have already attained VA status—in the form of statutory benefits. The average annual amount paid to current veterans or survivors under various benefits programs included $9,811 for disability compensations; $8,509 for pensions; $13,612 for dependency and indemnity compensations; and $3,829 for death pensions.[43] Additionally, the Veterans Health Administration's (VHA) FY 2007 budget for health care and research was over $37 billion.

As previously indicated, the demand for benefits and health care is sure to rise, given the hundreds of thousands of service men and women still serving in Iraq and Afghanistan. Currently 860,000 service members who have fought in Iraq and Afghanistan remain in the military and have yet to begin claiming VA benefits or demanding VA health care. This number does not include many hundreds of thousands of soldiers, sailors, airmen, marines and coast guardsmen who are deployed elsewhere, who will also be entitled to long-term VA care and benefits, albeit with less severe needs. Nor does it include the hundreds of thousands more who are expected to serve in both Iraq and Afghanistan before U.S. involvement in these conflicts is over.

Despite the Department of Defense's attempts to reduce the number of soldiers reported injured in Iraq and Afghanistan by maintaining two separate books for combat-related and noncombat-related injuries, the latter injuries are nonetheless real, and will have high costs associated with them in the future. All veterans injured while in service, regardless of how their service-related injuries were incurred, are eligible for disability pensions and other benefits including medical treatment, long-term health care, education grants, housing assistance, reintegration assistance, and counseling. All these benefits have budgetary consequences for which the government has failed to plan.[44]

Linda Bilmes and Joe Stiglitz point out:

> Each of the over 1.7 [currently 1.8] million troops deployed in Iraq and Afghanistan (and the hundreds of thousands more who are expected to serve before the conflicts are over) are potentially eligible to claim disability compensation from the Veterans Benefit Administration. Disability compensation is money paid to veterans with "service-connected disabilities"—meaning that the disability was the result of illness, disease, or injury incurred or aggravated while the person was on active military service.

According to Bilmes and Stiglitz, the estimated costs of providing health care and disability benefits to today's returning service members is immense. Bilmes and Stiglitz's "conservative scenario" estimates that the U.S. government will spend some $422 billion for health care and disability benefits over the course of Iraq and Afghanistan veterans' lives. Their "realistic-moderate scenario" was significantly higher. It reached a staggering $717 billion—nearly three quarters of a trillion dollars.[45] Additionally, Stiglitz and Bilmes noted that the VA will not be the only federal government agency that will face incremental costs as a result of these service members' injuries, because many of these service members will be unable to obtain jobs that provide family health care benefits. As a result,

Medicaid and other federal agencies are likely to pick up at least part of the tab.

In order to avert America's looming crisis in veterans affairs, the 111th Congress and the Obama administration must correct the mistakes of the Bush administration's short-sighted veteran policy. Recognizing the significant cracks in the VA system outlined in the previous chapters, and the long-term costs associated with reforming that system and augmenting its capacity, lawmakers must fulfill our nation's promise to those who defend our country. To do any less is to break our moral contract with our veterans and endanger our nation's long-term security interests.

Notes

1. Report on the Rehabilitative Care and Administrative Processes at Walter Reed Army Medical Center and National Naval Medical Center, 17, http://national security.oversight.house.gov/documents/20070418170543.pdf.

2. RAND Corporation, "Invisible Wounds of War," 432, http://www.rand.org/pubs/monographs/2008/RAND_MG720.pdf.

3. Report on the Rehabilitative Care and Administrative Processes at Walter Reed Army Medical Center and National Naval Medical Center, 17.

4. RAND, "Invisible Wounds of War," 103.

5. Joseph Stiglitz and Linda Bilmes, *The Three Trillion Dollar War: The True Cost of the Iraq Conflict* (New York: W. W. Norton, 2008), 83.

6. RAND, "Invisible Wounds of War," 197. For methodology, please refer to RAND study.

7. Army Surgeon General, United States Army Medical Command, "Mental Health Advisory Team V," 46. http://www.armymedicine.army.mil/reports/mhat/mhat_v/MHAT_V_OIFandOEF-Redacted.pdf.

8. Ibid., 42.

9. Elizabeth Lorge, "Army Study Finds Delayed Combat Stress Reporting," U.S. Army, November 14, 2007, http://www.army.mil/-news/2007/11/14/6090-army-study-finds-delayed-combat-stress-reporting/.

10. Charles Milliken, Jennifer Auchterlonie, and Charles Hoge. "Longitudinal Assessment of Mental Health Problems Among Active and Reserve Component Soldiers Returning from the Iraq War," *The Journal of the American Medical Association* 298, no. 18 (2007): 2141–2148. http://jama.ama-assn.org/cgi/content/abstract/298/18/2141?maxtoshow=&HITS=10&hits=10&RESULTFORMAT=&fulltext=post-deployment&searchid=1&FIRSTINDEX=0&resourcetype=HWCIT; Luis Martinez, "More Returning Soldiers Cite Mental Health Issues," ABC News, November 17, 2007, http://abcnews.go.com/Politics/Story?id=3863079&page=1.

11. Thomas A. Grieger, Stephen J. Cozza, Robert J. Ursano, Charles Hoge, Patricia E. Martinez, Charles C. Engel, and Harold J. Wain, "Posttraumatic Stress Disorder and Depression in Battle Injured Soldiers," http://ajp.psychiatryonline.org/cgi/content/full/163/10/1777.

12. PBS *Frontline,* "The Soldier's Heart," http://www.pbs.org/wgbh/pages/frontline/shows/heart/.

13. Report on the Rehabilitative Care and Administrative Processes at Walter Reed Army Medical Center and National Naval Medical Center, 20.

14. Ibid.

15. RAND, "Invisible Wounds of War," 252.

16. PBS *Frontline,* "The Soldier's Heart."

17. Testimony of Sergeant Roy Meredith before the Senate Committee on Veterans Affairs, July 23, 2008, http://veterans.senate.gov/hearings.cfm?action=release.display&release_id=81a59ac4-42d6-48ab-a62e-a1c0d6f7c7dc.

18. Testimony of Dr. Joseph Scotti before the Senate Committee on Veterans Affairs, July 23, 2008, http://veterans.senate.gov/hearings.cfm?action=release.display&release_id=1e9911e2-3e6e-4f33-89b6-a80f9575d47a.

19. Department of Veterans Affairs, "National Center for PTSD Factsheet," http://www.ncptsd.va.gov/ncmain/ncdocs/fact_shts/fs_va_ptsd_programs.html.

20. Government Accountability Office, "DoD and VA: Preliminary Observations on Efforts to Improve Health Care and Disability Evaluations for Returning Service Members," September 26, 2007, 18, http://www.gao.gov/new.items/d071256t.pdf.

21. Ibid.

22. Report on the Rehabilitative Care and Administrative Processes at Walter Reed Army Medical Center and National Naval Medical Center, 24.

23. RAND Corporation, "Stop Loss: A Nation Weighs the Tangible Consequences of Invisible Combat Wounds," Summer 2008, http://www.rand.org/publications/randreview/issues/summer2008/wounds3.html.

24. RAND, "Invisible Wounds of War," 251.

25. Nick Lazaredes, "America's Forgotten Soldiers," SBS Dateline, http://www.gsfso.org/Forgotten_Soldiers-US_Veterans.html.

26. RAND, "Invisible Wounds of War," 265.

27. Report on the Rehabilitative Care and Administrative Processes at Walter Reed Army Medical Center and National Naval Medical Center, 20.

28. Deborah Warden, "TBI During Wartime: The Afghanistan and Iraq Experience," Presentation to the Second Federal Traumatic Brain Injury Interagency Conference, March 9, 2006, 21.

29. Stiglitz and Bilmes, *The Three Trillion Dollar War,* 66.

30. Ibid.

31. RAND, "Invisible Wounds of War," 439.

32. Report on the Rehabilitative Care and Administrative Processes at Walter Reed Army Medical Center and National Naval Medical Center, 16.

33. Veterans for America, "Trends in Treatment of America's Wounded Warriors," November 7, 2007, 6, http://www.veteransforamerica.org/wp-content/uploads/2008/04/07-226va_trends_in_treatment.pdf.

34. Ibid.

35. Ibid., 7.

36. Ibid.

37. Interview with retired health care professional formerly employed by the military. June 25. 2008.

38. Veterans for America, "Trends in Treatment of America's Wounded Warriors," 7.

39. Ibid., 7.

40. Report on the Rehabilitative Care and Administrative Processes at Walter Reed Army Medical Center and National Naval Medical Center, 17 (emphasis added).

41. Ibid., 22.

42. Ibid., 17.

43. Department of Veterans Affairs, "FY 07 VA Information Pamphlet," http://www1.va.gov/vetdata/docs/Pamphlet_2-1-08.pdf.

44. Stiglitz and Bilmes, *The Three Trillion Dollar War,* 63.

45. Ibid., 86–87.

CHAPTER 7

Conclusion

Lawrence J. Korb

On December 7, 2008, 67 years after the attack on Pearl Harbor, then President-elect Obama announced that he was nominating retired Army General Eric Shinseki to be his Secretary of Veterans Affairs. General Shinseki is the highest ranking military officer to head the VA since President Harry Truman tapped General Omar Bradley in August 1945.

In some respects, General Shinseki is an even more distinguished officer than General Bradley. After two years running the VA, General Bradley went on to become Army Chief of Staff. General Shinseki had already served as the Army Chief of Staff, holding that post from 1999–2003. Moreover, General Shinseki eagerly embraced the task of taking over the VA whereas Bradley was reluctant to take it on. Shinseki told Obama that he could think of no higher responsibility than ensuring that the men and women who have served our nation in uniform are treated with the care and respect that they have earned. In addition, unlike Bradley, Shinseki was actually wounded in war. He served two tours in Vietnam where he lost part of his foot and was the recipient of two purple hearts and three bronze stars.

Given this background, it was not surprising that another distinguished retired Army General, Colin Powell, who served as chairman of the Joint Chiefs of Staff for the first President Bush and as secretary of state for the second, called Shinseki's appointment inspired, or that the Iraq and Afghanistan Veterans of America said that General Shinseki is a person that "has always put patriotism ahead of politics and is held in high regard by veterans of Iraq and Afghanistan."

As has been made clear from the discussion in our previous chapters, General Shinseki, like General Bradley, will have his work cut out for him.

Like his distinguished predecessor, General Shinseki must retool the VA to meet the needs of a new generation of veterans. Since 2001, VA has seen approximately 350,000 veterans of the conflicts of Afghanistan and Iraq at its medical centers. This figure represents only about 40 percent of the total number of veterans of the wars who have been discharged from military service.

These numbers are sure to grow as the wars in Iraq and Afghanistan continue to drag on. According to the Status of Forces Agreement (SOFA) agreed to by the Bush administration and the Iraqi government, which went into effect on January 1, 2009, American troops will remain on the ground in Iraq at least until the end of 2011. And as the United States draws down its forces in Iraq, it is increasing its troop presence in Afghanistan significantly.

Moreover, as casualties in Iraq decline, they continue to increase markedly each year in Afghanistan. In 2008, over 150 Americans died in Afghanistan while another 2,500 have been wounded since the conflict began. Finally, according to Secretary of Defense Robert Gates, who has served both the Bush and Obama administrations as the Pentagon chief, the United States could remain in Iraq and Afghanistan for another 10 to 15 years.

In addition, the VA will have to deal with a much higher proportion of veterans suffering serious combat wounds, particularly head wounds. The ratio of wounded troops from Iraq who have survived serious injuries is much higher than in previous wars. That is, 15 injuries for every fatality compared to 2.6 and 2.0 for the Vietnam war and World War II, respectively.

General Shinseki, his team, and his successors will also have to cope with the vastly increased levels of psychological injuries that have resulted and will result from repeated and lengthy combat deployments. The Rand Corporation, the Pentagon's own research institution or think tank, estimates that as many as 300,000 Iraq and Afghanistan veterans, or about one out of every five troops deployed to either theatre, may be suffering from Posttraumatic Stress Disorder, or PTSD.

Unfortunately, only about half of the 20 percent of veterans with PTSD seek treatment. This is not surprising given the fact that James Peake, Shinseki's immediate predecessor, tried to downplay and trivialize the severity of this illness as, "what anyone who played football in their youth might have suffered."

The VA must also be retooled to deal with the increasing number of women veterans. As of the end of 2008, nearly 200,000 military women have been deployed to Iraq or Afghanistan at least once and in 2007 alone, the VA treated more than a quarter of a million women, a number that is expected to double within the next five years. In addition to the physical and psychological wounds experienced by their male counterparts, 15 percent of the female veterans from the wars in Iraq and Afghanistan who have sought treatment at the VA have screened positive for sexual trauma.

Like General Bradley, General Shinseki will have to alter the way that the VA does business if he wants to deal with these challenges. As we noted in Chapter 2, as soon as he took over the VA, General Bradley doubled the VA's field staff and increased the central office staff by 5,000. He also made sure that disabled combat veterans received priority in the VA hospitals and that all veterans were treated equally, whether they were members of such veterans' lobbying groups as the American Legion or the Veterans of Foreign Wars (VFW) or not. In his two years in office, Bradley changed the VA's image from a conservative organization serving World War I veterans to a dynamic organization more in harmony with its time.

To change the VA to an organization more in harmony with its times, especially after the failures of the Bush administration to plan for the costs of troops wounded physically and psychologically in the wars in Iraq and Afghanistan, General Shinseki will have a number of advantages.

First and foremost is his reputation as a highly decorated wounded soldier who was willing to speak the truth to power regardless of the consequences. Since leaving active duty in 2003, General Shinseki, an amputee, has worked frequently with wounded veterans. And in February 2003, in testimony before the Senate Armed Services Committee during the buildup to the invasion and occupation of Iraq, Shinseki contradicted the Bush administration's overoptimistic predictions about how many troops it would take to secure Iraq after Saddam Hussein had been removed from power.

General Shinseki, then serving as Army Chief of Staff, famously told Congress that it would take several hundred thousand troops to secure Iraq, rather than the 30,000 that the Bush administration had planned on. Although he was publicly ridiculed for this statement, by among others the then Deputy Secretary of Defense Paul Wolfowitz, who dodged the draft during the war in Vietnam, and was not supported publicly by any of his fellow members of the Joint Chiefs of Staff, Shinseki's warning proved prophetic. Had the president and his acolytes listened to Shinseki's advice, there would be far fewer wounded veterans to care for.

Second, General Shinseki will have the full support of President Barack Obama, the nation's commander in chief, who has shown not only that he understands the problems and challenges confronting the VA but is willing to spend political and financial capital on it. In announcing Shinseki's appointment immediately after naming his national security team, Obama said that he will remember the men and women who will make the greatest sacrifices to implement his national security strategy and that as a nation we must show them, and their families, the same devotion they have shown this country.

To accomplish these goals, President Obama promised to build a 21st century VA that will cut red tape, eliminate shortcomings, and will fully fund VA health care and VA benefits.

Obama also demonstrated that he is aware of the unique problems facing today's veterans. In his press conference announcing the Shinseki appointment, he noted that far too many veterans are suffering the signature injuries of the wars in Iraq and Afghanistan, namely PTSD and Traumatic Brain Injury (TBI), and that too few of them are receiving the treatment they need. Moreover, in the current economic climate, he wants the VA to do more to help these veterans find jobs that pay well, provide good benefits, and enable them to support their families.

Finally, the president concluded by stating that showing this devotion is not a favor to the veterans but rather a sacred trust to repay the favor they have done for us. But, as this volume has noted, accomplishing these goals is easier said than done. It will require a level of commitment by the president to the VA that few of his predecessors have demonstrated and a willingness to continue to spend a significant amount of political and financial capital throughout his tenure.

Third, the efforts to support and fully fund the VA will have the enthusiastic support of the American people and their electoral representatives, at least for the time being. Because such a small portion of the population has had to fight and bear the costs of the wars in Iraq and Afghanistan, Americans, regardless of their political affiliation, now agree that it is not only politically correct to help the wounded warriors but it is also a moral duty to do so.

But as this volume has demonstrated, this support could evaporate as the American people and their elected representatives focus on other issues that they feel are more pressing.

Index

Abizaid, John, 104

Agent Orange, 9, 36–42

Agent Orange Victims International, 38

Agent Orange: Vietnam's Deadly Fog, 37

Agent Orange Working Group, 39

Allen, George, 61

All-volunteer force (AVF), 1

Al-Maliki, Prime Minister, 7

American Consumer Satisfaction Index, 114

American Legion, 21, 25, 28, 33, 40, 55, 56, 157

American Psychiatric Association, 33

Army National Guard, 4, 58, 142

Arrears of Pension Act, 18–19

Atherton, Warren G., 28–29

Baucus, Max, 62

Benefit claims, veteran: complexity, increased, 132–34; VA outreach, 131–32; volume, 131

Benjamin, Mark, 3

Best Care Anywhere, 113

Bilmes, Linda, 104, 122, 133, 147, 151

Block, John R., 66

Bloomfield, Joseph, 17

Bonior, David, 39

Bonus Expeditionary Force, 23–24

Born on the Fourth of July, 34

Boston Globe, 58, 83

Bradley, Omar N., 30–31, 35, 155, 157

Brooke Army Medical Center, 128

Brooks, Jack, 67

Brown, Jesse, 74

Bullock, Alexander Hamilton, 18

Bureau of Pensions, 17, 19

Bush, George H. W., 40, 56, 62, 71

Bush, George W., 44, 58, 80–84

Butler, Stuart M., 76–77

Campbell, Alec, 52, 54, 63

Carmon, Douglas B., 129

Carr, William J., 95

Carter, Jimmy, 35

Centers for Disease Control, 39

Challenges of today's veterans: all-volunteer force, 1; educational/aptitude standards, lowering, 5–6; length of campaigns, 1–2; medical coverage, 4–5; medical problems, deployment and, 3; multiple deployment and inadequate rest, 2–3; nature of wars, 7; reserve component, 4; size of forces, 6–7; survival rate, 5; training, length of, 3; unit deployment *vs.* individual deployment, 6; women in combat, 5

Chambliss, Saxby, 61

Christian Science Monitor, 68

Civil War: Arrears of Pension Act, 18–19; benefits law, 17–18; Dependent Pension Act of 1890, 20; Grand Army of the Republic, 20; National Asylum for Disabled Volunteer Soldiers, 18; pension cost, 18–19; Sherwood Act of 1912, 20

Clark, Wesley, 60

Cleland, Max, 32, 33, 35–36, 37, 67, 69

Cleveland, Grover, 19–20
Clinical Practice Guidelines Index, 114
Clinton, Bill, 42, 70–79
Clinton, Hillary, 70
Cochran, John J., 22
Committee on World War Veterans'
  Legislation, 28
Coolidge, Calvin, 22
Crandell, William, 16
Cranston, Alan, 32, 33, 36
Crisis magazine, 23
Crow, James, 23, 29
Curtis, Charles, 23

Daschle, Tom, 39, 40, 41–42, 62, 83
Defense and Veterans Brain Injury Center
  (DVBIC), 150
Demographics of veterans: Global
  War on Terror veterans, 101; health
  care limitations, 95–96; multiple
  deployments, 105–6; Persian Gulf War
  veterans, 100–101; posttraumatic stress
  disorder, 106–8; racial, ethnic, sexual
  diversity, increase of, 101–2; strain
  on VA system, 93–96; veteran care,
  projecting future of, 102–10; veteran
  population, declining, 96–97; Vietnam
  veterans, 97, 98–99; World War II/
  Korea-era veterans, 97
Department of Defense, 2, 10, 37, 97, 150;
  administrative impediments to VA care,
  120–22; battlefield casualties, 102–4
Department of the Interior, 17
Department of Veterans Affairs, 30–31,
  40–41, 51, 52, 121, 150; budget of,
  54–55; cabinet level positions, 69–70;
  cabinet-level status, 63–70; Capitol Hill
  roles, 56–58; Clinton administration,
  70–79; separate entities of, 53; VA health
  care, accessing, 95–96; VoteVets, 60–61
Dependent Pension Act of 1890, 20
Dependent Pension Bill of 1887, 20
Derwinski, Edward, 40, 41, 56
DeVictor, Maude, 37, 38
Disabled Veterans of America, 25, 85
Dole, Robert, 34, 70, 79–80
Dole-Shalala Commission, 126, 128, 130
Dooley, Jim, 143

Dow Chemical, 37, 38
Dudley, W. W., 19

Economist magazine, 64
Edwards, Steve, 133
Eisenhower, Dwight, 30
Eliot, Charles W., 26
Environmental Protection Agency, 37, 38, 69
Erspamer, Gordon, 146

Facility Healthcare Effectiveness Data and
  Information Set, 114
Facility ORYX, 114
Farragut, David, 18
Federal Bureau for Vocational
  Rehabilitation, 21
Federal Recovery Coordinators (FRC), 128
Feingold-Sanders bill, 132
Fish, Hamilton, Jr., 22
Forbes, Charles R., 21
Ford, Gerald, 34
Frear, James, 23
Freedom of Information Act, 101
Frontline, 144

Gates, Robert, 44, 120, 156
Gay, Dan, 144
General Accounting Office, 39, 66–67
GI Bill of Rights: Korean, 31, 43;
  Montgomery GI Bill, 43–44, 58;
  post-9/11 GI Bill, 44, 58; Veterans'
  Educational Assistance Program, 43–44;
  World War II, 28–31
Gingrich, Newt, 70, 72–73, 74
Glassford, Pelham, 23
Global War on Terror (GWOT), 4, 6;
  veterans of, 101
Gore, Al, 71, 79–81
Government Accountability Office (GAO),
  122, 129
Grand Army of the Republic, 20
Grant, Ulysses S., 18
Gugliotta, Guy, 76
Gulf War Illness, 42, 101
Gulf War Syndrome (GWS), 100

Hagel, Chuck, 9, 36, 44
Haley, Sarah, 32

Hardie, Anthony, 101
Harding, Warren G., 21–22
Harrison, Benjamin, 20
Harrison, William Henry, 17
Hattaway, Doug, 81
Healthcare benefits, barriers to accessing:
   administrative impediments, 120–22;
   case management/continuity of care,
   127–29; claims backlog, 131–34;
   disability evaluations, DoD/VA, 122–24;
   DoD Physical Disability Evaluation
   System, 124–25; health care enrollment,
   116–17; increased demand, 115–18;
   information sharing, inadequate,
   129–30; measures of quality, 114–15;
   priority group rankings, 118–19;
   Schedule for Rating Disabilities,
   125–27; Veterans Health care Eligibility
   Reform Act of 1996, 115; waiting lists,
   119–20
Hegseth, Pete, 61
Heinz, John, 39, 69
Henderson, Thelton, 41
Heritage Foundation, 76–78
Hines, Frank, 21, 26, 30
Holsinger, James W. Jr., 62
Hoover, Herbert, 22, 23
House Veterans Affairs Committee, 33, 37,
   64, 73–74
Houston, David F., 21
Hussein, Saddam, 42, 157

Improvised Explosive Devices (IEDs),
   147–48
Independent Review Group, 120, 128, 141,
   145, 150
Institute of Medicine (IOM), 126
Iraq and Afghanistan Veterans of America
   (IAVA), 59–60, 85, 86, 155

Jeffords, Jim, 82
Johnson, Donald, 33–34
Johnson, Lyndon, 4, 70

Kerry, John, 40, 82–84
Kettle, Donald, 69
Kizer, Kenneth W., 71
Korean GI Bill, 31, 43

Korea veterans, 97
Kovic, Ron, 32, 34, 38
Kurtis, Bill, 37

LaFollette, Robert, 19
Laird, Melvin, 37
Lambro, Donald, 77
Lifton, Robert, 32–33
Lincoln, Abraham, 18
Longman, Phillip, 113, 114
Lou Gehrig's disease, 100

MacArthur, Douglas, 24
Magnuson, Warren, 35
May, Phillip, 33
McAllister, Bill, 73, 77
McCain, John, 61, 82, 84–86, 95
McCurry, Mike, 73
McGovern, George, 34
Meade, George, 18
Medical Evaluation Board (MEB), 125
Mellon, Andrew, 21
Mental health epidemics. *See also*
   Posttraumatic stress disorder (PTSD):
   long term outlook, 150–52; multiple/
   prolonged deployments, effects of,
   141–42; traumatic brain injuries, 140,
   147–50
Meredith, Roy, 144
Meshad, Shad, 33, 35
Mexican-American War, 17
MHAT V, 106, 142
Mikva, Abner, 37
Military and Veterans Initiatives at Easter
   Seals, 129
Monroe, James, 16
Montgomery, G. V. (Sonny), 40, 43, 64, 65,
   73–74
Montgomery GI Bill, 43–44, 58
Muller, Bobby, 32, 39

National Academy of Public Administration,
   66
National Asylum for Disabled Volunteer
   Soldiers, 18
National Cemetery Administration (NCA),
   53, 54
National Center for Policy Analysis, 71

National Home for Disabled Volunteer
    Soldiers, 18
National Institute of Medicine, 141
National Naval Medical Center, 128
National Resources Planning Board, 26
New England Journal of Medicine, 114
New York Times, 64, 66, 67, 68, 69, 72
Nimmo, Robert, 36, 39
Nixon, Richard, 33–34, 64

Obama, Barack, 56, 84–86, 152, 155,
    157–58
Office of Management and Budget (OMB),
    65
Office of the Surgeon General for the
    United States Army Medical Command,
    106, 142
Oliphant, Tom, 83
Operation Enduring Freedom, 101, 104
Operation Iraqi Freedom, 101, 104
Owens, Charlie, 37

Palin, Sarah, 85
Panetta, Leon, 73
Panic of 1819, 17
Partnership for Veterans Health Care
    Benefit Reform, 83
Patman, Wright, 22, 24
Patton, George, 24
Peake, James, 156
Pensions, 17–20; Arrears of Pension Act,
    18–19; Bureau of Pensions, 17, 19; cost
    of, 18–19; Dependent Pension Act of
    1890, 20; Dependent Pension Bill of
    1887, 20
Persian Gulf War, 5, 100–101
Philadelphia Inquirer, 81
Physical Disability Evaluation System
    (PDES), 124–25
Physical Evaluation Board (PEB), 125
Politics (American), veterans' impact on:
    cabinet level status, 51–52, 63–70;
    Capitol Hill influence, 55–63; Clinton
    administration, 70–79; Heritage
    Foundation, 76–78; presidential
    campaigns, 1996–2008, 79–86; VA
    system, 52–55; veterans issues, 63
Porter, John Edward, 66

Post-Deployment Health Assessment
    (PDHA), 142–44
Post-Deployment Health Reassessment
    (PDHRA), 143–44
Post-9/11 GI Bill, 44, 58, 59–60
Posttraumatic stress disorder (PTSD), 99;
    access/quality of care, gaps in, 145;
    delayed onset, underestimation of
    problem, 142–43; demographics of,
    106–8; denying the problem, 146–47;
    Guard /Reserves studies, 144–45;
    multiple/prolonged deployments,
    141–42; PDHA/PDHRA problems,
    143–44; scope of problem, 141; social
    and cultural barriers, 146; Vietnam
    veterans, 33, 37
Postwar Manpower Conference (PMC),
    26–27
Powell, Colin, 2, 155
President's Commission on Care for
    America's Returning Wounded Warriors,
    108
Prevention Index II, 114
Principi, Anthony J., 83, 95
Project VetVoice, 85

RAND Corporation, 107, 141, 145, 147,
    156
Rankin, John, 28–29
Reagan, Ronald, 36, 64–66
Research Advisory Committee on Gulf War
    Veterans' Illness, 101
Retooling, Veterans
    Administration, 155–58
Reutershan, Paul, 38
Revolutionary War, 16–17
Rieckhoff, Paul, 59
Roberts, Ray, 35
Roosevelt, Franklin Delano, 8, 24, 25–27,
    70
Roosevelt, Theodore, 15, 56
Roudebush, Richard L., 34
Ryan, Michael, 39

Safire, William, 64, 67, 70, 72
St. Petersburg Times, 57, 68–69, 75
Salon magazine, 3
Sarasota Herald Tribune, 86

Schedule for Rating Disabilities (VASRD), 125–27

Schmidt, Steve, 82

Scotti, Joseph, 144–45

Selective Training and Service Act of 1940, 25

Senate Armed Services Committee, 157

Senate Governmental Affairs Committee, 69

Senate Veterans' Affairs Committee, 144

Senior Oversight Committee, 128, 130

Servicemen's Readjustment Act, 29

Shatan, Chaim, 32–33

Sherwood Act of 1912, 20

Shinseki, Eric, 13, 155–58

Sholzen, John, 66

Sisters of Charity of Nazareth Health System, 99

Skocpol, Theda, 17

Smith, Dale, 109

Smith, Jack, 34–35

Smith, William, 17

Solomon, Gerald B., 64, 65, 72

Soltz, Jon, 60, 61

Spaulding, Frank, 26

Status of Forces Agreement (SOFA), 156

Steering Committee on the Health Related Effects of Herbicides, 38

Stelle, John, 30

Stigletz, Joseph, 122, 133, 147, 151

Stockman, David, 36, 51, 65

Stump, Bob, 74

Sullivan, Paul, 133

Talking Points Memo, 86

Task Force on Returning Global War on Terror Heroes, 130

Task Force to Improve Health Care Delivery for Our Nation's Veterans, 130

Thomas, Elbert, 25, 27

Thompson, Mark, 3

Thurmond, Strom, 51

Time magazine, 3

Tocqueville, Alexis de, 55

Tombstone Bonus, 22

Traumatic brain injuries (TBI), 107; access/quality of care, gaps in, 150; identifying/diagnosing, 148–49; scope of problem, 147–48

Troxler, Howard, 75

Truman, Harry S., 30, 155

Tucker, Michael, 149

Turnage, Thomas K., 69

U.S.-Iraqi Status of Forces Agreement (SOFA), 101

USA Today, 108

Van Thieu, Nguyen, 34

VA Office of the Inspector General, 119–20

VA Schedule for Rating Disabilities (VASRD), 123

Veterans Administration. *See* Department of Veterans Affairs

Veterans Administration retooling, 155–58

Veterans Affairs, history of. *See also* GI Bill of Rights: Civil War, 17–20; Mexican-American War, 17; pensions, 17–20; providing benefits, political controversy of, 15–17; Revolutionary War to War of 1812, 16–17; Vietnam war, 31–42; World War I, 20–24; World War II, 25–31

Veterans' Affairs Committee, 33, 35

Veterans Affairs' National Center for PTSD, 145

Veterans' Agent Orange Disabilities Act of 1987, 40

Veterans Benefit Administration (VBA), 53–54, 102, 121

Veterans Bureau, 21

Veterans' Dioxin and Radiation Exposure Act, 40, 41

Veterans' Disability Benefits Commission Report, 130

Veterans Disability Commission, 126

Veterans' Educational Assistance Program, 43–44

Veterans for America (VFA), 60, 85, 148

Veterans for Common Sense, 101, 133, 146

Veterans Health Administration (VHA), 53, 121, 150

Veterans Health Care Authorization Act, 132

Veterans Healthcare Eligibility Reform Act of 1996, 115

Veterans Health Information Systems and Technology Architecture (VHISTA), 129

Veterans of Foreign Wars, 21, 25, 40, 79, 157; Capitol Hill roles, 55–58

Veterans of Modern Warfare, 101

Veterans' Readjustment Benefits Act of 1966, 31

Veterans United for Truth, 146

Vets for Freedom, 61–62

Vietnam Veteran Resocialization Unit, 33

Vietnam veterans, 97, 98–99

Vietnam Veterans Against the War, 32–33

Vietnam Veterans of America, 39, 41, 64

Vietnam Veterans of America Foundation (VVAF), 60

Vietnam Veterans' Outreach Program, 35

Vietnam Veterans' Psychological Readjustment Act, 35

Vietnam war, 31–42; Agent Orange, 36–42; posttraumatic stress disorder, 33, 37; Steering Committee on the Health Related Effects of Herbicides, 38; VA hospitals, 32; Vet Centers, 35–36; Veterans' Dioxin and Radiation Exposure Act, 40, 41; veterans of, 97, 98–99; Veterans' Readjustment Benefits Act of 1966, 31; Vietnam Veteran Resocialization Unit, 33; Vietnam Veterans Against the War, 32–33; Vietnam Veterans' Outreach Program, 35; Vietnam Veterans' Psychological Readjustment Act, 35

Villa, Pancho, 23

Vocational Rehabilitation Act of 1918, 20

VoteVets, 60–61, 85

Wagner, Robert, 28

Wallace, Henry, 25–26

Walter Reed Medical Center, 10, 87, 120–22, 128, 149

Walters, Harry, 69

Warrior Transition Units, 129

War Risk Insurance Act Amendments of 1917, 20

Washington, George, 1, 16

Washington, Terrill G., 75

Washington Post, 68, 71, 76, 77

Washington's Federal Triangle, 23–24

Washington Times, 73, 76

Waters, Walter W., 22–23

Webb, Jim, 9, 44, 61, 86

Wilkins, Roy, 23

Wilson, Woodrow, 21

Wolfowitz, Paul, 157

Women, combat restrictions placed on, 5

Woods, Timothy, 109

World War I: American Legion, 21; Bonus Expeditionary Force, 23–24; Tombstone Bonus, 22; Vocational Rehabilitation Act of 1918, 20; War Risk Insurance Act Amendments of 1917, 20

World War II: American Legion, 28; Committee on World War Veterans' Legislation, 28; GI Bill of Rights, 15–16, 28–31; National Resources Planning Board, 26; Postwar Manpower Conference, 26–27; Selective Training and Service Act of 1940, 25; Servicemen's Readjustment Act, 29; Veterans Administration, changes to, 30–31

World War II/Korea-era veterans, 97

Zeimer, Matthew, 3–4

Zumwalt, Elmo, 9

Zumwalt, Elmo, Jr., 41

Zumwalt, Elmo, III, 41

About the Authors

DR. LAWRENCE J. KORB is a Senior Fellow at the Center for American Progress and a Senior Advisor to the Center for Defense Information. Prior to joining the Center, he was a Senior Fellow and Director of National Security Studies at the Council on Foreign Relations. From July 1998 to October 2002, he was Council Vice President, Director of Studies, and holder of the Maurice Greenberg Chair. Prior to joining the Council, Mr. Korb served as Director of the Center for Public Policy Education and Senior Fellow in the Foreign Policy Studies Program at the Brookings Institution, Dean of the Graduate School of Public and International Affairs at the University of Pittsburgh, Vice President of Corporate Operations at the Raytheon Company, and Director of Defense Policy Studies at the American Enterprise Institute. Mr. Korb Served as Assistant Secretary of Defense (Manpower, Reserve Affairs, Installations and Logistics) from 1981 through 1985. In that position, he administered about 70 percent of the Defense budget. For his service in that position, he was awarded the Department of Defense's medal for Distinguished Public Service. Dr. Korb served on active duty for four years as a Naval Flight Officer, and retired from the Naval Reserve with the rank of Captain.

SEAN E. DUGGAN is a Research Associate for National Security at the Center for American Progress. He works primarily on military affairs and other related U.S. foreign policy and international security issues. Duggan's work has been featured in the *Washington Post,* the *Los Angeles Times* and the *Boston Globe.* Duggan has also been published in *The Nation,* the Johns Hopkins University's *Transatlantic Relations Journal,* and *Political Science and Politics Magazine.* He coauthored the Center's latest report, "How to Redeploy" (September 2008). Before joining American Progress in 2006, Duggan spent a year studying in Cadiz, Spain and graduated from the Henry M. Jackson School of International Studies at the University of Washington in 2005 with a degree in foreign policy, diplomacy, peace and security studies. Sean is a native of Seattle, Washington.

PETER M. JUUL is a research associate for National Security at the Center for American Progress, where he works extensively on military affairs and U.S. national security policy. He holds a bachelor's degree in Political Science/International Affairs from Carleton College in Northfield, Minnesota, and a master's degree in Security Studies from Georgetown University in Washington, D.C. A native of Minnesota, he currently resides in Arlington, Virginia.

MAX A. BERGMANN is the Deputy Policy Director at the National Security Network, a think tank in Washington DC. Bergmann has worked extensively on military affairs and ethnic conflict. Bergmann has been published by the *New Republic,* the *American Prospect,* the *Los Angeles Times,* the *Boston Globe,* the *Philadelphia Inquirer, the New York Times,* the *Washington Times,* and the *Bulletin of the Atomic Scientists.* He received his master's degree in Comparative Politics from the London School of Economics and his B.A. from Bates College.